MIXED
METHODOLOGY

Applied Social Research Methods Series
Volume 46

APPLIED SOCIAL RESEARCH
METHODS SERIES

Series Editors
LEONARD BICKMAN, Peabody College, Vanderbilt University, Nashville
DEBRA J. ROG, Vanderbilt University, Washington, DC

Other volumes in this series are listed at the back of the book

MIXED METHODOLOGY

Combining Qualitative and Quantitative Approaches

Abbas Tashakkori
Charles Teddlie

Applied Social Research Methods Series
Volume 46

SAGE Publications
International Educational and Professional Publisher
Thousand Oaks   London   New Delhi

For information:

SAGE Publications, Inc.
2455 Teller Road
Thousand Oaks, California 91320
E-mail: order@sagepub.com

SAGE Publications Ltd.
6 Bonhill Street
London EC2A 4PU
United Kingdom

SAGE Publications India Pvt. Ltd.
M-32 Market
Greater Kailash I
New Delhi 110 048 India

Printed in the United States of America

Library of Congress Cataloging-in-Publication Data

Tashakkori, Abbas.
 Mixed methodology: combining qualitative and quantitative
approaches / by Abbas Tashakkori and Charles Teddlie.
  p. cm. -- (Applied social research methods; v. 46)
 Includes bibliographical references and index.
 ISBN 0-7619-0070-5 (cloth : alk. paper)
 ISBN 0-7619-0071-3 (pbk. : alk. paper)
 1. Social sciences--Research--Methodology. I. Teddlie, Charles.
II. Title. III. Series: Applied social research methods series ; v. 46.
 H62 .T247 1998
 300'.72--ddc21

                              98-9042

This book is printed on acid-free paper.
  99 00 01 02 03 04 10 9 8 7 6 5 4 3

Acquisition Editor:	C. Deborah Laughton
Editorial Assistant:	Eileen Carr
Production Editor:	Wendy Westgate
Editorial Assistant:	Denise Santoyo
Typesetter/Designer:	Rose Tylak

To our wives,
Marylyn and Susan,

and our children,
Cyrus, Mitra, Katie, and Timmy

Contents

Preface

This volume is an addition to the rapidly growing area of interest in research methodology: the study of *mixed method* and *mixed model studies*. Although several authors are now writing about these methods in a variety of fields, there is a lack of conceptual clarity in many of their articles and chapters, and they often do not give concrete examples of the methods that are being used. The unique contributions of this volume are twofold: (a) We create a logically exhaustive typology of mixed models and mixed method studies, and (b) we present a "how-to" guide for each of the major types of studies.

While authors are writing about these new methods in various fields, scholars in the mainstream *quantitative tradition* (the positivists and post-positivists) and *qualitative tradition* (the constructivists) have *not* embraced mixed model studies. For example, a noted "bible" of post-positivism (Cook & Campbell, 1979) mentioned mixed methods only when discussing the monomethod bias. Similarly, the *Handbook of Qualitative Research* (Denzin & Lincoln, 1994) had only one chapter (on clinical research methods) that directly addressed mixed methods.

A mainstream mixed method literature is now developing in a variety of fields, but few authors have attempted to develop taxonomies of these methods (e.g., Creswell, 1995; Miller & Crabtree, 1994; Morse, 1991). Some of the fields and subfields in the social and behavioral sciences in which mixed methods have been called for include education, evaluation, nursing, public health, sociology, clinical research, administration sciences, community psychology, women's studies, and school effectiveness research.

There are similarities across the mixed method and mixed model studies employed in these diverse fields. In Part I of this volume, we develop a logical taxonomy of both mixed method and mixed model studies, pointing out the similarities in the methods that we perceive across these diverse fields. We make a distinction between mixed methods and mixed models. Mixed methods combine qualitative and quantitative approaches in the methodology of a study (such as in the data collection stage), while mixed model studies combine these two approaches across all phases of the research process (such as conceptualization, data collection, data analysis, and inference). After an intensive review of the literature, we believe that mixed model studies are the growing trend in the social and behavioral sciences.

In Part II of this volume, we present the methods and strategies of mixed method and mixed model research (e.g., sampling, measurement, data collection, data analysis). In this part, we first summarize traditional approaches to these topics and then demonstrate how researchers have mixed the techniques when doing their research. Examples of unique mixed methodological approaches from a variety of fields are presented in this section. In selecting these examples, we have been nonjudgmental regarding the overall soundness or strength of the research. They are presented to provide illustrations of the current methods in various fields. Also, we were able to find hundreds of studies in various disciplines that could be classified as mixed. Only a few could be presented here.

Part III presents simple and extended examples of mixed model designs. To increase the relevance of the book to graduate students (or to those who are using mixed studies for the first time), several of these examples involve the recent dissertations of our students. Most of these dissertations used either *sequential* or *parallel mixed methods* in which the two basic approaches are used alternatively or together to examine the same phenomenon. These examples provide more information on precisely how these dissertation (and other) studies are put together.

We believe that the study of mixed methods and mixed model research is in its infancy, and that the growth of the field has been retarded to date by the vestiges of the paradigm wars, which are revisited in Part I of this volume. Now that these wars are behind us, researchers are free to use the methods most appropriate to their research question. Also, we believe that research should be done with a clear intent to answer a question, solve a problem, or evaluate a program. We stress the importance and predominance of the research question over the paradigm, and we encourage researchers to use appropriate methods from both approaches to answer their research question. For most applications in the social and behavioral sciences, these research questions are best answered with mixed method or mixed model research designs rather than with a sole reliance on either the quantitative or the qualitative approach.

Acknowledgments

We are indebted to our families, colleagues, and students, who provided us with support and served as sounding boards during the writing of this book. We would like to express our appreciation to Marylyn Sines for editorial assistance, Professor Spencer Maxcy for comments on the first part of the book, Mindy Crain-Dorough for library assistance, and Sharareh Nikbakht for preparing illustrations and graphs.

Part I

Paradigms and Politics of Research

This part discusses the paradigms and politics of research in the social and behavioral sciences. Chapters 1 and 2 review major issues in the paradigm wars, which are debates over the relative merits of opposing worldviews or belief systems; in the social and behavioral sciences, these have typically been between positivism and constructivism. An alternative paradigm, pragmatism, is presented in Chapter 1 and expanded upon in Chapter 2. Chapter 2 further distinguishes among four major scientific paradigms (logical positivism, postpositivism, pragmatism, constructivism).

The chapters in this section describe a taxonomy of methodological approaches for the social and behavioral sciences, including monomethods, traditionally defined mixed methods, and a different orientation toward combining the quantitative and qualitative approaches, which we call mixed model studies. Mixed methods combine the qualitative and quantitative approaches to the research methods of a study, while mixed model studies combine these two approaches across all phases of the research process.

Chapter 3 presents a new taxonomy of mixed model studies based on differences in three major research stages (i.e., determination of questions/hypotheses, data gathering and research operations, analyses and inferences). This new taxonomy serves as the organizational rubric for the rest of the book.

1

Introduction to Mixed Method and Mixed Model Studies in the Social and Behavioral Sciences

PARADIGM WARS AND MIXED METHODOLOGIES

Examples of the Wars

During the past three decades, several debates or "wars" (e.g., Datta, 1994; Gage, 1989; Guba & Lincoln, 1994; House, 1994; Rossi, 1994) have raged in the social and behavioral sciences regarding the superiority of one or the other of the two major social science paradigms or models. These two models are known alternately as the *positivist/empiricist* approach or the *constructivist/phenomenological* orientation (e.g., Cherryholmes, 1992; Guba & Lincoln, 1994).

Paradigms may be defined as the worldviews or belief systems that guide researchers (Guba & Lincoln, 1994). The importance currently attributed to paradigms in the social and behavioral sciences derives from Kuhn's (1970) influential book titled *The Structure of Scientific Revolutions.* In this book, he argues that paradigms are the models that are imitated within any given field, and that competing paradigms may exist simultaneously, especially within immature sciences (Kneller, 1984; Kuhn, 1970).

The positivist paradigm underlies what are called *quantitative methods,* while the constructivist paradigm underlies *qualitative methods* (e.g., Guba & Lincoln, 1994; Howe, 1988; Lincoln & Guba, 1985). Therefore, the debate between these two paradigms has sometimes been called the qualitative-quantitative debate (e.g., Reichardt & Rallis, 1994). The abbreviations QUANs (for those preferring the quantitative point of view) and QUALs (for those preferring the qualitative point of view) have been used in describing participants in these debates or "wars" (e.g., Creswell, 1995; Morse, 1991).

These *paradigm wars* have been fought across several "battlefields" concerning important conceptual issues, such as the "nature of reality" or the "possibility of causal linkages." No discipline in the social and behavioral sciences has avoided manifestations of these paradigm wars. Datta (1994) called the participants in such wars *wrestlers;* we prefer to use the term *warriors.*

"Warriors" from education include Lincoln and Guba (1985), who have contended that the tenets of positivism and the quantitative methodology that accompanies that paradigm have been discredited. These authors also contend that constructivism and qualitative methods are in ascendance. Smith and Heshusius (1986), also writing in the field of education, suggested "shutting down" the dialogue between the two camps, saying that their incompatibility made further dialogue unproductive. This point of view has been called the *incompatibility thesis.*

Likewise in psychology, the 1970s and 1980s witnessed important methodological debates between scholars such as Cronbach (1982) and Cook and Campbell (1979). These debates focused on the relative importance of internal validity (emphasizing *controlled settings,* which were considered sacrosanct by the positivists) and external validity (emphasizing *natural settings,* which were preferred by the constructivists). Gergen (1973) posed the question, "Is a science of social psychology possible?" challenging the tenets of positivism that underpinned that subarea of psychology, especially the possibility of making time- and context-free generalizations.

Similarly in anthropology, Gardner (1993) criticized Margaret Mead's anthropological work in Samoa for its overreliance on preconceived notions and naive acceptance of the reports of key informants. These responses are typical criticisms of the positivist camp toward the constructivists (or "naturalists").

A final example of these wars comes from the applied area of evaluation research. As noted by Datta (1994), the "dialogues" of three successive presidents of the American Evaluation Association (Fetterman, 1992; Lincoln, 1991; Sechrest, 1991) were very stringent in their defense of their own methodological positions and in their attack on the position of the "other side." Although such debate may have been inevitable, it became increasingly unproductive during the 1980s and early 1990s.

The End of the Paradigm Wars and
the Emergence of Mixed Methods

There have been numerous attempts in the social and behavioral sciences to make peace between the two major paradigmatic positions. "Pacifists" have appeared who state that qualitative and quantitative methods are, indeed, compatible. In education and evaluation research (e.g., Howe, 1988; Reichardt & Rallis, 1994), authors have presented the compatibility thesis based on a different paradigm, which some have called *pragmatism*. Thus we may refer to the pacifists in the paradigm wars as *pragmatists*.

At this time, the paradigm debates have primary relevance within the history of social science philosophy because many active theorists and researchers have adopted the tenets of *paradigm relativism,* or the use of whatever philosophical and/or methodological approach works for the particular research problem under study (e.g., Howe, 1988; Reichardt & Rallis, 1994). Even some of the most noted warriors (i.e., Guba & Lincoln, 1994) have signaled an end to the wars, stating,

> The metaphor of paradigm wars described by Gage (1989) is undoubtedly overdrawn. Describing the discussions and altercations of the past decade or two as wars paints the matter as more confrontational than necessary. A resolution of paradigm differences can occur only when a new paradigm emerges that is more informed and sophisticated than any existing one. That is most likely to occur if and when proponents of these several points of view come together to discuss their differences. (p. 116)

Pragmatically oriented theorists and researchers now refer to "mixed methods" (or mixed methodology or methodological mixes), which contain elements of both the quantitative and qualitative approaches (e.g., Brewer & Hunter, 1989; Patton, 1990). For instance, Greene, Caracelli, and Graham (1989) presented 57 studies that employed mixed methods, and described the design characteristics of these mixed studies. Specific types of mixed methods will be discussed later in this chapter.

The Current State of Affairs

We accept the assumptions implicit within paradigm relativism and assume that the paradigm wars are over, having been superseded by the pragmatist orientation briefly described above. As noted by Brewer and Hunter (1989), most major areas of research in the social and behavioral sciences now use multiple methods as a matter of course: "Since the fifties, the social sciences have grown tremendously. And with that growth, there is now virtually no major problem-area that is studied exclusively within one method" (p. 22).

The detente in the paradigm wars has been positive for research development in many fields because most researchers now use whatever method is appropriate for their studies, instead of relying on one method exclusively. Nevertheless, pragmatists have often employed imprecise language in describing their methodologies, using some rather generic terms (e.g., *mixed methods*) to connote several different ways of conducting a study or a series of studies. Datta (1994) recently referred to what she called "mixed-up models" that derived from the "lack of a worldview, paradigm, or theory for mixed-model studies," concluding that "such a theory has yet to be fully articulated" (p. 59).

We don't pretend to present such a formal theory for mixed method and mixed model studies in this brief volume, but we do hope to offer some guidelines for more systematically conceptualizing such studies. Before introducing our taxonomy of mixed method and mixed model studies, however, we briefly describe some of the major issues related to the paradigm wars and their resolution in the next section of this chapter.

MORE DETAILS REGARDING
THE PARADIGM WARS

The following section is intended for readers unfamiliar with the issues that were debated during the paradigm wars and how they were resolved to the satisfaction of much of the social scientific community. This brief historical review of the paradigm wars is not a treatise on the philosophy of science but is a "Cook's tour" through the paradigm wars and their aftermath. Those familiar with these issues may wish to skip this section.

The historical importance of these debates is partially illustrated by their longevity. Hammersley (1992) has noted that debates about quantitative and qualitative research actually have roots in the mid-nineteenth century and occurred in sociology in the 1920s and 1930s. Recent attention to the debate started with a revival of the fortunes of qualitative research methods in the 1960s in sociology and psychology, which had been dominated by quantitative methods (i.e., survey or experiment) throughout the 1940s and 1950s (Hammersley, 1992).

Although there are the two major opposing points of view, it is apparent that several philosophical orientations, or paradigms, have been posited and defended (e.g., Greene, 1994; Guba, 1990; Guba & Lincoln, 1994). We refer to four philosophical orientations: logical positivism, postpositivism, pragmatism, and constructivism (other variants of which are known as interpretivism, naturalism, and so on). We have chosen these orientations because they represent aspects of what we consider to be major stages in the paradigm debates: (a) the debunking of logical positivism after World War II, (b) the pervasiveness of the postpositivist position, (c) the ascendance of constructivism, followed by the paradigm wars, and (d) pragmatism and the compatibility thesis. Each of these stages is briefly described in the next four sections of this chapter.

The Debunking of Logical Positivism After World War II

Positivism (also called logical positivism) has origins dating back to nineteenth-century French philosopher August Comte. Positivism bases knowledge solely on observable facts and rejects speculation about "ultimate origins." Lincoln and Guba (1985) ascribed several "axioms" to positivism:

1. *Ontology* (nature of reality): Positivists believe that there is a single reality.
2. *Epistemology* (the relationship of the knower to the known): Positivists believe that the knower and the known are independent.
3. *Axiology* (role of values in inquiry): Positivists believe that inquiry is value-free.
4. *Generalizations:* Positivists believe that time- and context-free generalizations are possible.
5. *Causal linkages:* Positivists believe that there are real causes that are temporally precedent to or simultaneous with effects.

We will add a sixth distinction noted by many authors (e.g., Goetz & LeCompte, 1984; Patton, 1990):

6. *Deductive logic:* There is an emphasis on arguing from the general to the particular, or an emphasis on a priori hypotheses (or theory).

Logical positivism was discredited as a philosophy of science after World War II (e.g., Howe, 1988; Phillips, 1990; Reichardt & Rallis, 1994). Dissatisfaction with the axioms of positivism (especially with regard to ontology, epistemology, and axiology) became increasingly widespread throughout the social and behavioral sciences during the 1950s and 1960s, giving rise to *postpositivism.* As Guba and Lincoln (1994) have noted, postpositivism is the intellectual heir to positivism and has addressed several of the more widely discredited tenets of positivism.

The Pervasiveness of the Postpositivist Position

Landmark works of postpositivism (e.g., Hanson, 1958; Popper, 1959) appeared in the late 1950s, and they quickly gained widespread credibility throughout the social scientific community. Postpositivism was a reaction to the widely discredited axioms of positivism, and many of its tenets were in direct opposition to those of its predecessor.

While many QUANs continued to follow the tenets of positivism in the 1950s and 1960s, Reichardt and Rallis (1994) convincingly contended that some of the most influential quantitative methodologists of that period (e.g., Campbell & Stanley, 1966) were "unabashedly postpositivist" in their orientation. According to Reichardt and Rallis, these quantitative methodologists were postpositivists because their writings indicated that they agreed with the following tenets of that philosophy:

- *Value-ladenness of inquiry:* Research is influenced by the values of investigators.
- *Theory-ladenness of facts:* Research is influenced by the theory or hypotheses or framework that an investigator uses.
- *Nature of reality:* Our understanding of reality is constructed. (See Chapter 2 for a further discussion of these issues.)

These postpositivist tenets are currently shared by both qualitatively and quantitatively oriented researchers because they better reflect common understandings regarding both the "nature of reality" and the conduct of social and behavioral research in the second half of the twentieth century. Reichardt and Rallis (1994) concluded that postpositivism more accurately characterizes contemporary quantitative inquiry than does logical positivism, noting that there is a quantitatively oriented postpositivist camp that includes some of the best known quantitative researchers of the 1960s and 1970s.

For example, the experimental psychologist Rosenthal (1976) discussed at length what was called the experimenter effect: The way the experimenter looks, feels, or acts may unintentionally affect the results of a study. Cook and Campbell (1979), who were certainly quantitatively oriented, acknowledged experimenter bias as a threat to the validity of studies. This experimenter bias is a good example of a methodological flaw that might result in facts that are value- or theory-laden (basic tenets of postpositivism). Cook and Campbell (1979), in a discussion of causation in the social sciences, stated,

We share the postpositivists' belief that observations are theory-laden and that the construction of sophisticated scientific apparatus and procedures for data presentation often involve the explicit or implicit acceptance of well developed scientific theories, over and beyond the theory being tested. (p. 24)

Similarly, experimental social psychologists (e.g., Jones & Davis, 1966; Jones & Nisbett, 1972) explored and discussed dispositional attributions, which involve actor-observer differences in perception. They speculated on whether or not the testing of personality theory may be heavily influenced by the personal attributions (including values) of the researchers doing the work. Again, this is an example of researchers using traditional experimental methods and quantitative data who were actively exploring and discussing postpositivist tenets, such as the value-ladenness of facts.

Thus quantitative methodologists wrote about and provided empirical evidence for some of the tenets of postpositivism in the 1960-1980 time period. While these methodologists held assumptions associated with postpositivism, it is important to remember that they worked within a tradition that emphasized "methodological correctness" (Smith, 1994). When choices came down between the qualitative or quantitative orientations, these methodologists weighed in on the side of the experimental design, which characterizes traditional positivism. For example, Cook and Campbell (1979), in a spirited response to critics of their validity distinctions, concluded, "We assume that readers believe that causal inference is important and that experimentation is one of the most useful, if not *the* most useful, way of gaining knowledge about cause" (p. 91, italics in the original).

It is clear from a reading of this section of their well-known 1979 book that they prefer experimental (or quasi-experimental) work, value internal validity very highly, and believe that causal inferences are possible under certain heavily prescribed circumstances.

The Ascendance of Constructivism, Followed by the Paradigm Wars

The discrediting of positivism resulted in the increasing popularity of paradigms more "radical" than postpositivism. These paradigms have several names (constructivism, interpretivism, naturalism), with constructivism being the most popular. Theorists associated with these paradigms borrowed from postpositivism but then added dimensions of their own to the models (e.g., Denzin, 1992; Gergen, 1985; Goodman, 1984;

Hammersley, 1989; LeCompte & Preissle, 1993; Schwandt, 1994). Some of these theorists were not content to see positivism, postpositivism, and their own philosophical orientation peacefully coexisting, believing that they had to argue for the superiority of their own paradigm to overcome the biases associated with the deeply embedded traditions of positivism and postpositivism. For example, Lincoln and Guba (1985) criticized one well-known quantitative methodologist for his attempts toward reconciliation of these points of view:

> Some scholars insist that postpositivism is nothing more than an over-reaction, and that it is time for a rapprochement that realigns positivism with the relativism that characterizes postpositivism. One such writer is Donald T. Campbell, who suggests that it is time to move into a post-postpositivist era, in which positivism and postpositivism are married off and live happily ever after. (p. 32)

Lincoln and Guba then set up a series of contrasts between the positivist and naturalist (their version of constructivism) paradigms that made such a "marriage" between them impossible. Referring back to the five axioms of positivism described above, they posited the following five axioms of the naturalist paradigm.

1. *Ontology* (nature of reality): Naturalists believe that there are multiple, constructed realities.
2. *Epistemology* (the relationship of the knower to the known): Naturalists believe that the knower and the known are inseparable.
3. *Axiology* (the role of values in inquiry): Naturalists believe that inquiry is value-bound.
4. *Generalizations:* Naturalists believe that time- and context-free generalizations are not possible.
5. *Causal linkages:* Naturalists believe that it is impossible to distinguish causes from effects.

As indicated above, we will add a sixth distinction noted by many authors:

6. *Inductive logic:* There is an emphasis on arguing from the particular to the general, or an emphasis on "grounded" theory.

Given such black-and-white contrasts, it was inevitable that paradigm wars would break out between individuals convinced of what Smith (1994) has called the "paradigm purity" of their own position. For example, Guba (1987) stated that one paradigm precludes the other "just as surely as the belief in a round world precludes belief in a flat one" (p. 31). Guba and Lincoln (1990, 1994) have repeatedly emphasized the differences in ontology, epistemology, and axiology that exist among the paradigms, thus fueling the paradigm wars. Smith (1983) stated the incompatibility thesis as follows:

> One approach takes a subject-object position on the relationship to subject matter; the other takes a subject-subject position. One separates facts and values, while the other sees them as inextricably mixed. One searches for laws, and the other seeks understanding. These positions do not seem compatible. (p. 12)

Paradigm "purists" have further posited the incompatibility thesis with regard to research methods: Compatibility between quantitative and qualitative methods is impossible due to the incompatibility of the paradigms that underlie the methods. According to these theorists, researchers who try to combine the two methods are doomed to failure due to the inherent differences in the philosophies underlying them.

Pragmatism and the Compatibility Thesis

Many influential researchers have stated that the differences between the two paradigms have been overdrawn, and that the schism is not as wide as has been portrayed by "purists." For example, House (1994) concluded that this dichotomization springs from a "misunderstanding of science," as he pointed out strengths and weaknesses of both the positivist and the constructivist traditions. House further contended that there "is no guaranteed methodological path to the promised land" (pp. 20-21).

There are a number of good reasons to declare detente in the paradigm wars. For example, writing within the evaluation discipline, Datta (1994) has given five convincing, practical reasons for "coexistence" between the two methodologies and their underlying paradigms:

- Both paradigms have, in fact, been used for years.
- Many evaluators and researchers have urged using both paradigms.
- Funding agencies have supported both paradigms.
- Both paradigms have influenced policy.
- So much has been taught by both paradigms.

On a philosophical level, pragmatists had to counter the incompatibility thesis of the paradigm warriors, which was predicated upon the link between epistemology and method. To counter this paradigm-method link, Howe (1988) posited the use of a different paradigm: pragmatism. Cherry-holmes (1992) and Murphy (1990) have traced the roots of pragmatism to such American scholars as C. S. Peirce, William James, and John Dewey, with more contemporary theorists including W. V .O. Quine, Richard Rorty, and Donald Davidson. The philosophy has been identified almost exclusively with its place of origin (the United States), and European scholars have been somewhat disdainful of pragmatism due to its debunking of metaphysical concepts, such as truth (e.g., Nielsen, 1991; Rorty, 1990). Instead of searching for metaphysical truths, pragmatists consider truth to be "what works." Howe (1988) summarized this orientation as follows:

> After all, much of pragmatic philosophy (e.g., Davidson, 1973; Rorty, 1982; Wittgenstein, 1958) is *deconstructive*—an attempt to get philosophers to stop taking concepts such as "truth," "reality," and "conceptual scheme," turning them into superconcepts such as "Truth," "Reality," and "Conceptual Scheme," and generating insoluble pseudoproblems in the process. (p. 15, italics in the original)

A major tenet of Howe's concept of pragmatism was that quantitative and qualitative methods *are compatible*. Thus, because the paradigm says that these methods are compatible, investigators could make use of both of them in their research. Brewer and Hunter (1989) made essentially the same point:

> However, the pragmatism of employing multiple research methods to study the same general problem by posing different specific questions has some pragmatic implications for social theory. Rather than being wed to a particular theoretical style . . . and its most compatible method, one might instead combine methods that would encourage or even require integration of different theoretical perspectives to interpret the data. (p. 74)

Reichardt and Rallis (1994) have gone even further in their analysis of the compatibility of what they call "qualitative and quantitative inquiries." They contend that there are enough similarities in fundamental values between the QUANs and the QUALs to "form an enduring partnership" (Reichardt & Rallis, 1994, p. 85). These similarities in fundamental values include belief in the value-ladenness of inquiry, belief in the theory-ladenness of facts, belief that reality is multiple and constructed, belief in the fallibility of knowledge, and belief in the underdetermination of theory by fact.

The first three of these beliefs were discussed earlier in this chapter. Reichardt and Rallis (1994) contend that QUANs also believe (along with QUALs) that knowledge is fallible, quoting Cook and Campbell (1979): "We cannot prove a theory or other causal proposition" (Reichardt & Rallis, 1994, p. 22). The authors further contend that the QUANs and QUALs agree with the *principle of the underdetermination of theory by fact,* that is, that "any given set of data can be explained by many theories" (Reichardt & Rallis, 1994, p. 88). Reichardt and Rallis also listed other shared ideologies in the field of evaluation between QUANs and QUALs concerning the importance of understanding and improving the human condition, the importance of communicating results to inform decisions, the belief "that the world is complex and stratified and often difficult to understand" (p. 89).

Thus it can be argued that there is a common set of beliefs that many social and behavioral scientists have that undergird a paradigm distinct from positivism or postpositivism or constructivism, which has been labeled pragmatism. This paradigm allows for the use of mixed methods in social and behavioral research.

THE EVOLUTION OF METHODOLOGICAL APPROACHES IN THE SOCIAL AND BEHAVIORAL SCIENCES

Thus there is growing agreement among many social and behavioral scientists concerning the basic assumptions that underlie the philosophical orientation of pragmatism. Now that these philosophical issues have been addressed, we can turn our attention to specific methodological issues associated with mixed method and mixed model studies.

A wide variety of writers from different disciplines (e.g., Blalock, 1978; Brewer & Hunter, 1989; Datta, 1994; Patton, 1990) have been calling for more coherence in our descriptions of the different methodologies that we now have at our disposal in the social and behavioral sciences. Brewer and Hunter (1989) have specifically called for a more integrated methodological approach, focusing on the need for individual researchers (and research teams) to combine methods in their investigations.

Part of that methodological integration involves having more precision in the language that we use to describe multiple methods. The novice researcher is faced with a bewildering array of names for the methods employed in the social and behavioral sciences: *monomethods* (quantitative and qualitative, plus all variants therein), multiple methods, *mixed methods,* multimethod research, *triangulation* of methods, methodological mixes, and so on. In this section, we will present a taxonomy of methodological approaches, including a brief review of the evolution of those methods.

The taxonomy of methodological approaches in the social and behavioral sciences is presented in Table 1.1. There are three broad categories: monomethods (dating from the emergence of the social sciences in the nineteenth century through the 1950s), mixed methods (emerging in the 1960s and becoming more common in the 1980s), and mixed model studies (emerging as a separate type in the 1990s but having earlier precursors).

General Stages in the Evolution of Methodological Approaches in the Social and Behavioral Sciences

We will argue in this section that there has been an evolution in the social and behavioral sciences from the use of monomethods to the use of what we call mixed model studies. There are three general points to be made in this discussion: (a) The evolution first involved the acceptance of the use of mixed methods, (b) the evolution then involved the application of the distinctions that emerged during the paradigm wars to all phases of the research process, and (c) this evolution has occurred during the past 30 years at an ever increasing pace.

The First Stage of the Evolution: From Monomethods to Mixed Methods

This involved going from the use of one basic scientific method only to the use of a variety of methods. Thus, in Table 1.1, this involved the movement from Period I to Period II. The paradigm wars and their denouement through pragmatism and the compatibility thesis resulted in this transition. The history of this process has been discussed in previous sections of this chapter. A more complete description of the different types of pure and mixed methods will be presented in Chapters 2 and 3.

Table 1.1

The Evolution of Methodological Approaches
in the Social and Behavioral Sciences

Period I: The Monomethod or "Purist" Era
(circa the nineteenth century through 1950s)
- A. The Purely Quantitative Orientation
    - 1. Single Data Source (QUAN)
    - 2. Within One Paradigm/Model, Multiple Data Sources
        - a. Sequential (QUAN/QUAN)
        - b. Parallel/Simultaneous (QUAN + QUAN)
- B. The Purely Qualitative Orientation
    - 1. Single Data Source (QUAL)
    - 2. Within One Paradigm/Method, Multiple Data Sources
        - a. Sequential (QUAL/QUAL)
        - b. Parallel/Simultaneous (QUAL + QUAL)

Period II: The Emergence of Mixed Methods
(circa the 1960s to 1980s)
- A. Equivalent Status Designs (across both paradigms/methods)
    - 1. Sequential (i.e., two-phase sequential studies)
        - a. QUAL/QUAN
        - b. QUAN/QUAL
    - 2. Parallel/Simultaneous
        - a. QUAL + QUAN
        - b. QUAN + QUAL
- B. Dominant-Less Dominant Designs (across both paradigms/methods)
    - 1. Sequential
        - a. QUAL/quan
        - b. QUAN/qual
    - 2. Parallel/Simultaneous
        - a. QUAL + quan
        - b. QUAN + qual
- C. Designs With Multilevel Use of Approaches

Period III: The Emergence of Mixed Model Studies
(circa the 1990s)
- A. Single Application Within Stage of Study[*]
    - 1. Type of Inquiry—QUAL or QUAN
    - 2. Data Collection/Operations—QUAL or QUAN
    - 3. Analysis/Inferences—QUAL or QUAN
- B. Multiple Applications Within Stage of Study[**]
    - 1. Type of Inquiry—QUAL and/or QUAN
    - 2. Data Collection/Operations—QUAL and/or QUAN
    - 3. Analysis/Inferences—QUAL and/or QUAN

---

[*]There must be a mixing such that each approach appears in at least one stage of the study.

[**]There must be a mixing such that both approaches appear in at least one stage of the study.

The Second Stage of the Evolution:
From Mixed Method to Mixed Model Studies

This involved moving from the consideration of distinctions in method alone to the consideration of distinctions in all phases of the research process. As indicated in Table 1.1, this involved the movement from Period II to Period III. While the emergence of multiple methods typically has been treated as a methodological issue only, the linking of epistemology to method during the paradigm wars made it necessary to consider how different orientations affect other phases of the research process (e.g., the framing of the problem, the design of the study, the analysis of the data, the interpretation of the data). As Howe (1988) concluded, "The quantitative-qualitative distinction is applied at various levels: data, design and analysis, interpretation of results, and epistemological paradigm" (p. 15).

Creswell (1995) asked a basic question regarding this application of the paradigm-method link to other phases of the research process:

> The most efficient use of both paradigms would suggest another step toward combining designs: Can aspects of the design process other than methods—such as the introduction to a study, the literature and theory, the purpose statement, and research questions—also be drawn from different paradigms in a single study? (p. 176)

His answer was in the affirmative and he gave examples of how different paradigms or points of view could be applied to these phases of the research process.

Similarly, Brewer and Hunter (1989) applied their multimethod approach to all phases of the research process, not only to the measurement phase. Their phases included the formulation of the problem, the building and testing of theory, sampling, data collection/analysis, and reporting. They concluded,

> The decision to adopt a multimethod approach to measurement affects not only measurement but all stages of research. Indeed, multiple measurement is often introduced explicitly to solve problems at other stages of the research process. . . . These wider effects . . . of . . . multimethod tactics need to be examined in detail, including the new challenges that the use of multiple methods poses for data analysis, for writing and evaluating research articles for publication, and for doing research in an ethical manner. (Brewer & Hunter, 1989, p. 21)

In Chapter 3, we will explicitly apply the different philosophical approaches to several phases of a research project (determination of questions/hypotheses, data gathering and research operations, analyses, and inferences) using a taxonomy initially developed by Patton (1990). Indeed, this application will serve as the organizing framework for the remainder of this volume.

The Escalation of the Evolutionary Process

This evolutionary process toward the use of mixed method and mixed model studies has been occurring at an ever increasing pace during the past 30 years due to (a) the introduction of a variety of new methodological tools (both quantitative and qualitative), (b) the rapid development of new technologies (computer hardware and software) to access and use those methodological tools more easily, and (c) the increase in communication across the social and behavioral sciences.

A Taxonomy of Studies With Different Methodological Approaches

Three major types of studies are summarized in Table 1.1: monomethod studies, mixed method studies, and mixed model studies. Each of these basic types of studies is further divided into subcategories. In this section, we will provide brief definitions of these different methodological approaches; more detail with regard to their development and application will be forthcoming in Chapter 3.

Monomethod Studies

Monomethod studies are studies conducted by "purists" working exclusively within one of the predominant paradigms. Of course, the subdividing of the monomethod studies into the purely qualitative and the purely quantitative should come as no surprise to the reader. In Chapter 2, we will present examples of these pure designs, which are becoming increasingly rare in the social and behavioral sciences.

Mixed Method Studies

Mixed method studies are those that combine the qualitative and quantitative approaches into the research methodology of a single study or multiphased study. These methods are further subdivided into the five specific types of designs that are listed in Table 1.1.

All of the mixed method designs in Table 1.1 use triangulation techniques. These *triangulation techniques* evolved from the pioneer work of Campbell and Fiske (1959), who used more than one quantitative method to measure a psychological trait, a technique that they called the multi-method-multitrait matrix. Denzin (1978) described four different types of triangulation methods, including data triangulation, investigator triangulation, theory triangulation, and methodological triangulation. Methodological triangulation involves the use of both qualitative and quantitative methods and data to study the same phenomena within the same study or in different complementary studies. Patton (1990), in an influential book on evaluation methods, gave extensive examples of these four types of triangulation.

Creswell (1995) used the following distinctions in defining four of the mixed method designs that are presented in Table 1.1:

- *Sequential studies* (or what Creswell calls two-phase studies): The researcher first conducts a qualitative phase of a study and then a quantitative phase, or vice versa. The two phases are separate.

- *Parallel/simultaneous studies:* The researcher conducts the qualitative and quantitative phase at the same time.

- *Equivalent status designs:* The researcher conducts the study using both the quantitative and the qualitative approaches about equally to understand the phenomenon under study.

- *Dominant-less dominant studies:* The researcher conducts the study "within a single dominant paradigm with a small component of the overall study drawn from an alternative design" (Creswell, 1995, p. 177).

We have defined a fifth type of mixed method design, presented in Table 1.1:

- *Designs with multilevel use of approaches:* Researchers use different types of methods at different levels of data aggregation. For example, data could be analyzed quantitatively at the student level, qualitatively at the class level, quantitatively at the school level, and qualitatively at the district level.

Coincidentally, Miller and Crabtree (1994) presented a set of what they called "tools" for multimethod clinical research that closely resemble the types of studies that Creswell defined. They listed the following mixed method designs: *concurrent design* (analogous to parallel/simultaneous studies), *nested designs* (similar to dominant-less dominant studies), *sequential design* (analogous to sequential studies), and *combination design* (some combination of the above design options). Their work followed up on that of Stange and Zyzanski (1989), who were among the first to call for the integration of qualitative and quantitative research methods in clinical practice in the medical sciences.

Mixed Model Studies

The category that we designate as *mixed model studies* in Table 1.1 was defined as "mixed methodology designs" by Creswell (1995), who described them as follows: "This design represents the highest degree of mixing paradigms . . . The researcher would mix aspects of the qualitative and quantitative paradigm at all or many . . . steps" (pp. 177-178).

Our definition of mixed model studies is somewhat different: *These are studies that are products of the pragmatist paradigm and that combine the qualitative and quantitative approaches within different phases of the research process.* There may be single applications within phases of the study, such as a quantitative (experimental) design, followed by qualitative data collection, followed by quantitative analysis after the data are converted. In this application, the qualitative data would be converted to numbers using the "quantitizing" technique described by Miles and Huberman (1994).

There could also be multiple applications within phases of the study, such as the following:

- A research design that calls for a field experiment and extensive ethnographic interviewing to occur simultaneously and in an integrated manner
- Data collection that includes closed-ended items with numerical responses as well as open-ended items on the same survey (e.g., Tashakkori, Aghajanian, & Mehryar, 1996)
- Data analysis that includes factor analysis of Likert scaled items from one portion of a survey, plus use of the constant comparative method (e.g., Glaser & Strauss, 1967; Lincoln & Guba, 1985) to analyze narrative responses to open-ended questions theoretically linked to the Likert scales

The remainder of this volume includes descriptions of several types (see Table 3.1 in Chapter 3) of these mixed model studies and how to design them.

2

Pragmatism and the Choice of Research Strategy

In Chapter 1, we presented an overview of "mixed model studies" as an effort to combine the quantitative and qualitative approaches. We discuss these "mixed model studies" in Chapter 3. In the current chapter, we discuss a variety of conceptual and methodological issues pertaining to monomethod research.

The specific purposes of this chapter are to (a) discuss the relative importance of the research question, method, and paradigm, and present further distinctions among positivism, postpositivism, constructivism, and pragmatism; (b) present arguments for why pragmatism is the appropriate paradigm for justifying the use of mixed method and mixed model studies in the behavioral and social sciences; (c) present the basic issues and principles involved in traditional (monomethod) research procedures and provide more detail about the evolution of the taxonomy of methodological approaches presented in Table 1.1; and (d) provide more information about the differences and similarities among these methodological approaches.

If you are already familiar with distinctions among the paradigms, or you are not interested in paradigmatic discussions, there is no need to read the first two sections of the chapter. Please proceed to the last two sections of the chapter that concern design issues in monomethod research and a taxonomy of traditional data collection techniques.

THE DICTATORSHIP OF THE RESEARCH QUESTION (NOT THE PARADIGM OR METHOD)

For researchers, an important philosophical issue concerns the relative importance of paradigms, research methods, and research questions. In their most recent writing, Guba and Lincoln (1994) have reiterated that, from their point of view, research methods are of secondary importance to research paradigms:

> Both qualitative and quantitative methods may be used appropriately with any research paradigm. Questions of method are secondary to questions of paradigm, which we define as the basic belief system or worldview that guides the investigation, not only in choices of method but in ontologically and epistemologically fundamental ways. (p. 105)

Despite this statement, Guba and Lincoln continue to link specific paradigms with specific methods; for instance, they (1994) linked postpositivism with the following methodologies: "modified experimental/manipulative; critical multiplism; falsification of hypotheses; may include qualitative methods." On the other hand, they linked constructivism with a methodology that they called the "hermeneutical/dialectical" (p. 109).[1]

Howe (1988) states the pragmatist response to the importance of paradigm (and of the paradigm-methodology link) as follows:

> But why should paradigms determine the kind of work one may do with inquiry any more than the amount of illumination should determine where one may conduct a search? . . . Eschewing this kind of "tyranny of method" (Bernstein, 1983)—of the epistemological over the practical, of the conceptual over the empirical—is the hallmark of pragmatic philosophy. (p. 13)

Howe's (1988) comments follow up on the following admonition by Trow (1957): "Let us be done with the arguments of 'participant observation' versus interviewing . . . and get on with the business of attacking our problems with the widest array of conceptual and methodological tools that we possess and they demand" (p. 35).

Similarly, Brewer and Hunter (1989) stated that the multimethod approach allows investigators to "attack a research problem with an arsenal of methods that have nonoverlapping weaknesses in addition to their complementary strengths" (p. 17).

To put all of this more simply and directly, we believe that pragmatists consider the research question to be more important than either the method they use or the worldview that is supposed to underlie the method. Most good researchers prefer addressing their research questions with any methodological tool available, using the pragmatist credo of "what works" (e.g., Cherryholmes, 1992; Howe, 1988; Rorty, 1982). For most researchers committed to the thorough study of a research problem, method is secondary to the research question itself, and the underlying worldview hardly enters the picture, except in the most abstract sense. While the majority of this text thus far has concerned the paradigm wars and their resolution, it is important to reiterate that such paradigmatic considerations are not as important in the final analysis as the research questions that you are attempting to answer. (For a detailed presentation of types of research questions, see Hedrick, Bickman, & Rog, 1993, pp. 23-34.)

Our best scholars have always been more interested in investigating the questions that they have posed than the specific methodologies that they employ and the paradigms that underlie these methods. For instance, shortly after the recent death of pioneering methodologist Donald T. Campbell, Gene V. Glass eulogized him in a message sent out over the World Wide Web: "The method must follow the question. Campbell, many decades ago, promoted the concept of triangulation—that every method has its limitations, and multiple methods are usually needed."

COMPARISONS AMONG THE PARADIGMS

Table 2.1 contains a presentation of what we consider to be the primary distinctions among four major paradigms used in the social and behavioral sciences: positivism, postpositivism, pragmatism, and constructivism. The comparisons with regard to positivism, postpositivism, and constructivism were abstracted from Denzin and Lincoln (1994), Lincoln and Guba (1985), Guba and Lincoln (1990, 1994), House (1994), Greene (1994), and Miles and Huberman (1994). The information with regard to pragmatism was abstracted from Cherryholmes (1992), Greene (1994), House (1994), Howe (1988), Murphy (1990), and Rorty (1982). (Critical theory and its variants were not included in this comparison because they emphasize historical methods, while the focus in this text is on examination of ongoing phenomena.)

It is interesting to note that theorists delineating between positivism (including postpositivism) and constructivism (or interpretivism) typically do not include pragmatism as a third point of comparison (e.g., Guba & Lincoln, 1994; Smith & Heshusius, 1986), even though those two competing points of view do not exhaust the paradigmatic possibilities. As Howe (1988) notes, "This seems to be a serious omission, for pragmatists were largely responsible for bringing down positivism and would clearly reject the forced choice between the interpretivist and positivist paradigms" (p. 13).

Rejection of the Either-Or

In Table 2.1, the pragmatist point of view is illustrated as rejecting the forced choice between positivism (including postpositivism) and construc-

Table 2.1

Comparisons of Four Important Paradigms
Used in the Social and Behavioral Sciences

Paradigm	Positivism	Postpositivism	Pragmatism	Constructivism
Methods	Quantitative	Primarily Quantitative	Quantitative + Qualitative	Qualitative
Logic	Deductive	Primarily Deductive	Deductive + Inductive	Inductive
Epistemology	Objective point of view. Knower and known are dualism.	Modified dualism. Findings probably objectively "true."	Both objective and subjective points of view.	Subjective point of view. Knower and known are inseparable.
Axiology	Inquiry is value-free.	Inquiry involves values, but they may be controlled.	Values play a large role in interpreting results.	Inquiry is value-bound.
Ontology	Naive realism	Critical or transcendental realism.	Accept external reality. Choose explanations that best produce desired outcomes.	Relativism
Causal linkages	Real causes temporally precedent to or simultaneous with effects.	There are some lawful, reasonably stable relationships among social phenomena. These may be known imperfectly. Causes are identifiable in a probabilistic sense that changes over time.	There may be causal relationships, but we will never be able to pin them down.	All entities simultaneously shaping each other. It's impossible to distinguish causes from effects.

tivism with regard to methods, logic, and epistemology. In each case, pragmatism rejects the either-or of the incompatibility thesis and embraces both points of view. Nielsen (1991) suggests that pragmatism is a "reactive, debunking philosophy" (p. 164) that argues against dominant systematic philosophies, making mocking critiques of metaphysical assertions such as "the grand Either-Or."

With regard to methods, we discuss the pragmatist orientation toward using both qualitative and quantitative methods throughout this volume. While information in Table 2.1 indicates that postpositivists may also use qualitative methods, the discussion of methodological correctness in Chapter 1 should be reiterated. When choices are between qualitative or quantitative methodology, postpositivists typically prefer the experimental design (or variants thereof such as *quasi-experimental designs* and *ex post facto or causal comparative designs*) due to their concern with causality and internal validity (e.g., Cook & Campbell, 1979).

Similarly, constructivists prefer their own methods and dutifully distinguish the differences in methodological orientations. For example, Denzin and Lincoln (1994), writing in the *Handbook of Qualitative Research,* presented the following typologies of what they consider to be nonoverlapping methodologies:

> The five points of difference described above . . . reflect commitments to different styles of research, different epistemologies, and different forms of representation. Each work tradition is governed by a different set of genres. . . . Qualitative researchers use ethnographic prose, historical narratives, first-person accounts, still photographs, life histories, fictionalized facts, and biographical and autobiographical materials, among others. Quantitative researchers use mathematical models, statistical tables, and graphs. (p. 6)

Pragmatists, on the other hand, believe that either method is useful, choosing to use the dazzling array of both qualitative and quantitative methods listed by Denzin and Lincoln. Decisions regarding the use of either qualitative or quantitative methods (or both) depend upon the research question as it is currently posed and the phase of the research cycle that is ongoing.

The Research Cycle: Using Both Inductive and Deductive Logic

Research on any given question at any point in time falls somewhere within a cycle of inference processes, often referred to as the research cycle, the chain of reasoning (e.g., Krathwohl, 1993), or the cycle of scientific methodology. The cycle may be seen as moving from grounded results (facts, observations) through *inductive logic* to general inferences (abstract generalizations, or theory), then from those general inferences (or theory) through *deductive logic* to tentative hypotheses or predictions of particular events/outcomes. See Figure 2.1 for a visual representation of this chain of reasoning.

Research concerning any substantive area of inquiry travels through this cycle at least once before it ends. Research may start at any point in the cycle: Some researchers start from theories or abstract generalizations, while others start from observations. In many research reports, there is an initial attempt to inductively build a conceptual (theoretical) framework on

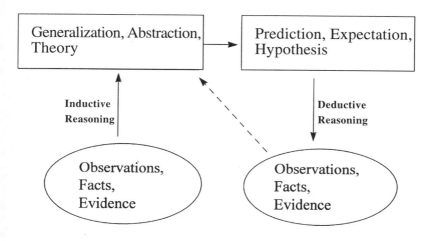

Figure 2.1. The Research Cycle (Cycle of Scientific Methodology)

the basis of previous findings (i.e., in the introduction section of a journal article). The obtained theoretical framework is then used as a basis for planning the course of the research. Regardless of where the researcher starts (facts or theories), a research project always starts because there is a question that needs a satisfactory answer, and partially travels through the cycle at least once.

At some points during the research process, it is likely that both types of inferences and methods will be used simultaneously. When this occurs, then we have the *mixed model studies with multiple applications within phase of study* depicted in Table 1.1 in Chapter 1. Pragmatists accept that they will have a choice of inductive and deductive logic in the course of conducting research on a question that needs to be answered.

Epistemological Relativism: The Use of
Both the Subjective and the Objective Points of View

Again, the black and white contrast of the incompatibility thesis (either a dualism or a singularity, either an objective or a subjective point of view) is challenged by the pragmatists' contention that scientific inquiry is not "formalistic" and that researchers may be both objective and subjective in epistemological orientation over the course of studying a research question. In this case, it is more reasonable to think of a continuum than two opposing poles: At some points, one may be more "subjective," while at others more "objective"; at some points the knower and the known must be interactive, while at others, one may more easily stand apart from what one is studying.

If one allows the researcher to use both qualitative and quantitative methodological tools, then this embrace of both the subjective and the objective points of view is inevitable.

The Roles of Values (Axiology)

As indicated in Table 2.1, positivists believe that inquiry is value-free, while constructivists believe that inquiry is value-bound. Postpositivists realize that values play an important role in inquiry, but they also believe that it is possible to control the degree to which values influence results and interpretations.

As noted in Chapter 1, postpositivists acknowledge both the value-ladenness and the theory-ladenness of facts (Reichardt & Rallis, 1994). Despite this recognition (and to a large degree *because of it*), postpositivists (e.g., Cook & Campbell, 1979) have devoted considerable effort to developing methods whereby the internal and external validity of their conclusions can be enhanced. These methods, aimed at enhancing the validity of results and their interpretations, represent the postpositivists' attempt to reduce the influence of their personal values and their allegiances to certain theoretical positions.

Pragmatists believe that values play a large role in conducting research and in drawing conclusions from their studies, and they see no reason to be particularly concerned about that influence. As Cherryholmes (1992) stated,

> For pragmatists, values and visions of human action and interaction precede a search for descriptions, theories, explanations, and narratives. Pragmatic research is driven by anticipated consequences. Pragmatic choices about what to research and how to go about it are conditioned by where we want to go in the broadest of senses. . . . Beginning with what he or she thinks is known and looking to the consequences he or she desires, our pragmatist would pick and choose how and what to research and what to do. (pp. 13-14)

Thus pragmatists decide what they want to research, guided by their personal value systems; that is, they study what they think is important to study. They then study the topic in a way that is congruent with their value system, including variables and units of analysis that they feel are the most appropriate for finding an answer to their research question. They also conduct their studies in anticipation of results that are congruent with their value system. This explanation of the way in which researchers conduct their research seems to describe the way that researchers in the social and behavioral sciences actually conduct their studies, especially research that has important social consequences.

Considerations of Ontology and Causality

The most controversial issues related to the positivist/postpositivist, constructivist, and pragmatist points of views concern ontology and causality (the last two rows in Table 2.1). Guba and Lincoln (1994) considered differences concerning the nature of reality (ontology) to constitute the defining distinction between positivism/postpositivism and constructivism: "The term *constructivism* denotes an alternative paradigm whose breakaway assumption is the move from ontological realism to ontological relativism" (p. 109, italics in original). Guba and Lincoln (1994) and Miles and Huberman (1994) defined the following types of realism:

(1) Naive realism. There is an objective, external reality upon which inquiry can agree (Guba & Lincoln, 1994, p. 111). As indicated in Table 2.1, this position is associated with positivists.

(2) Critical realism. There is an objective reality, but it can be understood only imperfectly and probabilistically (Guba & Lincoln, 1994, p. 111). This position is associated with postpositivists.

(3) Transcendental realism. This involves the belief that social phenomena exist in the objective world, and that there are some "lawful reasonably stable relationships" among them (Miles & Huberman, 1994, p. 429). This statement is an alternative expression of the postpositivist position.

(4) Ontological relativism. There are multiple social realities that are products of human intellects and that may change as their constructors change (Lincoln & Guba, 1994, p. 111). This position is associated with constructivists.

The major difference between the positivists/postpositivists and the constructivists on the nature of reality concerns the existence of an objective, external reality: The positivists/postpositivists believe that such an objective reality exists (please see Greenberg & Folger, 1988, chap. 1, for a discussion of controversies in this respect); the constructivists believe that only multiple, subjective realities exist.

The pragmatist point of view regarding reality consists of two parts:

1. There is an external world independent of our minds (Cherryholmes, 1992, p. 14). Thus the pragmatists agree with the positivists/postpositivists on the existence of this external reality.
2. On the other hand, pragmatists deny that "Truth" can be determined once and for all. They also are unsure if one explanation of reality is better than another. According to Cherryholmes (1992), the pragmatists' choice of one explanation over another "simply means that one approach is better than another at producing anticipated or desired outcomes" (p. 15).

Howe (1988) further explained the pragmatists' views regarding truth as follows:

> For pragmatists, "truth" is a normative concept, like "good," and "truth is what works" is best seen not as a theory or definition, but as the pragmatists' attempt to say something interesting about the nature of truth and to suggest, in particular, that knowledge claims cannot be totally abstracted from contingent beliefs, interests, and projects. (pp. 14-15)

Notions regarding causal relationships follow from these ontological distinctions. In short:

1. Postpositivists believe that there are some lawful, reasonably stable relationships among social phenomena that may be known imperfectly, or in probabilistic terms. Although the prediction of some event (criterion variables, "effects") from others (predictor variables, "causes", and so on) is never possible with 100% accuracy (probability of 1.00), the accuracy of predictions can be improved over time and as potent predictors are identified.
2. Pragmatists believe that there may be causal relationships but that we will never be able to completely pin them down.
3. Constructivists believe that all entities are simultaneously shaping each other and that it's impossible to distinguish causes from effects.

Thus there is an increase in pessimism regarding the possibility of understanding causal relationships as one goes from the postpositivists to the pragmatists to the constructivists. For example, House (1994), in a response to Cherryholmes' (1992) presentation of pragmatism, expressed the scientific realist (postpositivist) point of view as follows:

> Criteria for judging explanations vary from discipline to discipline and within disciplines from time to time, but with some contact with material reality. When scholars invent new ideas, using new stories and metaphors perhaps, they create new explanations of the physical world, but do not invent the world, which is already there. Nor is there any sense in which their explanations are finally "correct." No ultimate red light comes on. None is necessary. There are simply better explanations discussed by communities of scholars who have contact with material reality, which is always understood in language, concepts, and imagery. From this point, pragmatists seem overly pessimistic about the possibility of explaining the real world. (p. 18)

We feel somewhat conflicted between arguments of the postpositivist and pragmatist positions regarding the nature of reality and our ability to understand causal relationships. Both paradigms agree that there is an external reality and that we should explore causal relationships.

Both paradigms also agree on the principle of the underdetermination of theory by fact, that is, that the results from any data set can be explained by multiple theories (Reichardt & Rallis, 1994).

One group believes that we should strive for constantly better explanations of reality and causality, while the other believes that we should concur with those explanations of causality and reality that are closer to our own values because we will never be able to understand them absolutely. Given that there are multiple explanations of the results from any research study, the choice comes down to either the "better" explanation (postpositivist) or the explanation that is closer to the researchers' values (pragmatist). The choice between the "better" explanation and the one closer to the researcher's values will often be the same given that the researcher designed the study and gave the constructs their operational definitions.

The basic difference between the two viewpoints relates to optimism regarding finding the truth. On this issue, our position can best be described as cautiously optimistic pragmatism.

The Intuitive Appeal of Pragmatism

Given all these considerations, pragmatism appears to be the best paradigm for justifying the use of mixed method and mixed model studies

(Howe, 1988). Pragmatism is appealing (a) because it gives us a paradigm that philosophically embraces the use of mixed method and mixed model designs, (b) because it eschews the use of metaphysical concepts (Truth, Reality) that have caused much endless (and often useless) discussion and debate, and (c) because it presents a very practical and applied research philosophy: Study what interests and is of value to you, study it in the different ways that you deem appropriate, and use the results in ways that can bring about positive consequences within your value system.

DESIGN ISSUES ASSOCIATED
WITH MONOMETHOD APPROACHES

During the monomethod period (Period I, described in Table 1.1), there was a definite link between the methods used in a study and the scientific paradigm within which the investigator worked. As noted in Chapter 1, methodological purists believed in the incompatibility thesis, which prescribed that QUANs could not use qualitative methods, and vice versa.

Traditional monomethod research not only was expected to adhere to one of the two main approaches but also was expected to be uniquely different from the other approach in the type of data collection and data analysis procedures as well as in the types of inferences that were derived from these data analyses. The following discussion indicates that the two monomethods, in fact, have many similarities.

A Comparison of Monomethod Prototypes

There are two prototypical monomethod designs: (a) the *laboratory experiment,* characterized by a controlled research environment in which a manipulation of a variable occurs and involving confirmatory investigations of an a priori hypothesis, and (b) the *descriptive case study,* characterized by a natural environment in which no manipulation of any variable occurs and involving exploratory investigations.

These traditional research techniques have often been distinguished from each other on three major dimensions. The first dimension is the presence/absence of the *manipulation of* independent variables. The second dimension concerns the setting of the study *(natural setting* versus *controlled setting).* The third involves the presence/absence of prior hypotheses and/or predictions regarding the direction of findings.

BOX 2.1
The MAXMINCON Principle

In discussing the research design, Kerlinger (1986) summarizes different design issues in what he calls the *MAXMINCON* principle. Understanding the three components of the principle is a necessary step for doing research. The three components are to MAXimize the experimental variance, MINimize the error variance, and CONtrol the extraneous variance.

*MAX*imizing the experimental variance refers to the necessity of allowing enough difference between groups (or levels of an independent variable) to allow the effect to occur. For example, if two teaching methods are not different from each other, their differential effects are not detectable, even though they might be very effective. In Kerlinger's own language, "design, plan, and conduct research so that the experimental conditions are as different as possible" (p. 287).

*MIN*imizing the error variance provides power for detecting differences between groups or relationship between variables. These random fluctuations are similar to having constant fluctuating noise when you are trying to comprehend a conversation (signal). The greater the variation in noise, the more difficult it is to comprehend the signal. Error variance is the result of random fluctuations in reactions, behaviors, and/or measurement. Unreliability of measurement is one source of such error. Individual differences are another source. Usually, as the number of observations (sample size) increases, with this latter source, random errors cancel each other out.

*CON*trol of extraneous variables means that all competing variables that might affect the dependent variable should be removed (controlled). In the absence of such controls, one is unable to make inferences regarding the main independent variables of the study. For example, if gender is related to achievement along with teaching method, differences between groups of students might not be attributable to teaching method.

Although the MAXMINCON principle might seem more applicable to the experimental method than nonexperimental and/or qualitative methods, it is applicable to any research. The degree of one's confidence in a research finding regarding a relationship (what is called "internal validity" by QUANs) depends on the researcher's ability to rule out competing explanations for the results.

Much of the controversy over monomethod approaches revolves around the first two dimensions or, more specifically, the issues of manipulation and control. The *MAXMINCON Principle* of Kerlinger (1986) presents an excellent summary of these issues. It is described in Box 2.1.

Are the Two Monomethod Prototypes
Actually at Opposite Extremes?

As we discussed before, instead of posing either-or dichotomies when discussing research design issues, it is more productive to consider these issues as continua. For instance, it is more productive to consider the purely quantitative studies at one end of a continuum and the purely qualitative studies at the other end, with a wide variety of designs between. This preference for a continuum reflects the importance of looking at research design issues as shades of gray rather than as black or white. In fact, it is not even clear that the two research prototypes (experiment, case study) are actually that different from one another if you make one major assumption: that the purposes of both quantitative and qualitative research include answering how and why questions. (For a discussion regarding questions of causality, see Shadish, 1995.)

As indicated in Table 2.1, the philosophical positions concerning the possibility of making causal linkages range widely from the positivists to the constructivists. It is our position, however, that when it comes to the actual conduct of research studies, many researchers working within the qualitative case study tradition also try to answer causal questions. Just as many quantitatively oriented methodologists have adopted some of the tenets of constructivism, many qualitatively oriented methodologists believe that causal linkages are possible (see Shadish, 1995, for a review), although they are more cautious in making them due to the difficulties in controlling events in natural environments.

We do not believe that most researchers (using qualitative, quantitative, or mixed methods) are content merely to say that "something happened"; we believe that they want to explain how or why it happened. For instance, in the Whyte (1943) classic case study summarized in Box 2.2, he described causal relations among variables such as social structure, group structure, and career advancement. Yin (1993) convincingly argued that case studies should go beyond descriptive questions (who, what, where, how many, how much) to answer how and why questions (as do experiments and historical analysis, according to Yin).

Assuming that qualitative researchers are interested in studying causality, it is informative to compare purely quantitative studies and qualitative studies to see just how different or similar they are. We will now briefly compare laboratory experiments and descriptive case studies on the three dimensions used to distinguish them above: the manipulation of variables, the type of environment in which the study occurred (natural versus controlled), and the nature of the investigation (confirmatory versus

---

BOX 2.2
An Example of a Qualitative Case Study

Street Corner Society (1943), by William F. Whyte, has for decades been recommended reading in community sociology. The book is a classic example of a descriptive case study. Thus it traces the sequence of interpersonal events over time, describes a subculture that had rarely been the topic of previous study, and discovers key phenomena—such as the career advancement of lower income youths and their ability (or inability) to break neighborhood ties. The study has been highly regarded in spite of its being a single-case study, covering one neighborhood ("Cornerville") and a time period now nearly 50 years old. The value of the book is, paradoxically, its generalizability to issues on individual performance, group structure, and the social structure of neighborhoods. Later investigators have repeatedly found remnants of Cornerville in their work, even though they have studied different neighborhoods and different time periods.

SOURCE: From Yin (1993).

---

exploratory or a priori versus no a priori hypotheses). To set the stage, and also to provide a study to be compared with Whyte's research (Box 2.2), an example of a traditional quantitative confirmatory study (Latane & Rodin, 1969) is presented in Box 2.3.

Comparison of the Monomethod Prototypes: Manipulation of Variables

The traditional distinction between experiments and case/field studies states that experiments involve the manipulation of variables, while case studies do not. In fact, investigators conducting case studies often try to maximize the differences in the cases that they observe (the *MAX* in the *MAXMINCON* principle).

Experimental studies are usually categorized into laboratory, field, and natural experiments. The experimenter is the main agent of change in the independent variables in the first two types of experiments. In the third type, however, change in the independent variable happens as a result of other forces (social institutions, law, nature, and so on). The researcher's role is to compare the group and/or setting that has undergone such distinct change with groups or settings without such changes. While the "treatment" in case studies occurs through such "natural" manipulations, investigators often use qualitative sampling schemes (e.g., sampling extremes,

---

BOX 2.3
An Example of a Traditional
Quantitative Confirmatory Study

Latane and colleagues undertook a series of experiments in the late 1960s to further understand the phenomenon called "bystander intervention," which concerns the willingness of strangers to assist someone in distress. These experimental social psychologists became interested in this issue after a well-publicized case (i.e., the stabbing death of Kitty Genovese in New York City in 1964) in which a young woman was murdered while 38 of her neighbors watched but did nothing.

The researchers developed a theoretical position that predicted that the larger the number of "bystanders," the less likely it would be that a victim would receive help. They reasoned that noninterventions were acts of conformity: Individuals took their cues in responding to a victim's distress by observing others, and if the others did not help, this allowed them to interpret nonintervention as the appropriate behavior.

In one of their experiments, Latane and Rodin (1969) conducted an experimental situation around "a lady in distress": a female experimenter who staged an "accident" outside of the view of the subject, behind an unlocked collapsible curtain, but within the subject's hearing ranges. In the study, subjects heard a tape recording of the young woman climbing a chair, then falling, and then calling for help.

In one experimental condition, the subject was the only other person in the setting. In the other experimental condition, there was a "stooge," an accomplice of the experimenter who purposefully did not respond to the cries of the "victim." The theoretically derived prediction was supported: In the "alone" condition, 70% of the subjects responded to the "lady in distress," while in the "stooge" condition, only 20% of the subjects offered help.

---

maximum variance sampling) to highlight the differences between the groups they are studying. For instance, effective schools have been compared with ineffective schools to ascertain the differential impact that such schools have on students' learning (e.g., Brookover, Beady, Flood, Schweitzer, & Wisenbaker, 1979; Teddlie & Stringfield, 1993).

The major difference between case studies of very different groups and laboratory/field experiments using groups that have received different experimental treatments is that one involves a manipulation of nature and the other involves a manipulation conducted by the investigators. Such a methodological distinction does not seem to constitute a rigid dichotomy between case studies and experiments but a continuum from cases in which the investigator is the agent of change in the "treatment" to cases where the investigator has no control over such changes. (An extended example in Chapter 5 further illustrates the differences in control of "treatment" that different investigators can have when studying the same phenomenon.)

Comparison of the Monomethod Prototypes: Natural Versus Controlled Settings

The usual or traditional distinction between experiments and case studies states that experiments occur in controlled settings, while case studies occur in natural settings. From a research design perspective, the essence of this distinction concerns the control of extraneous variables (the *CON* component of the *MAXMINCON* principle) and the reduction of the error variance within treatment (the *MIN* component of the *MAXMINCON* principle).

Research conducted in controlled settings is more likely to have reduced the effect of extraneous variables and error variance than research conducted in natural settings. Nevertheless, there will always be uncontrollable variance, and even the best designed experiments will never eliminate all of it. In fact, conducting research in controlled settings can result in different types of extraneous variables, such as the *experimenter bias effect* (Rosenthal, 1976) in which experimenters' expectancies are somehow communicated to their subjects in a manner that affects their behavior.

On the other hand, well-designed case studies that include "controls" for important variables can yield results that are relatively devoid of the impact of extraneous variables and error variance. For instance, case studies comparing effective and ineffective schools have controlled for the following variables in their designs: the socioeconomic status of the students who attend the schools, the ethnic composition of the schools, the school district in which the study was conducted, the community type in which the study was conducted, the grade levels that are studied, the types of subject matter that is taught and tested, and other factors (e.g., Chrispeels, 1992; Hallinger & Murphy, 1986; Stringfield & Teddlie, 1990; Teddlie & Stringfield, 1993).

Of course, this discussion relates to the general issues of the internal and external validity of research studies, which will be discussed more thoroughly in Chapters 4 and 5. The point to be made here is that the distinction between natural settings and controlled settings is a continuum, not a rigid dichotomy, in terms of important issues such as the control of extraneous variables and error variance. Furthermore, experiments can occur in natural settings (field experiments) and case studies can occur in controlled settings (clinical case studies).

Comparison of the Monomethod Prototypes:
Confirmatory Versus Exploratory Investigations

The traditional distinction between experiments and case studies states that experiments are confirmatory in nature, involving the use of a priori hypotheses, while case studies are exploratory in nature and do not involve hypothesis testing. There are numerous counterexamples in which case studies did have a priori hypotheses and in which experiments did not.

This issue relates to the research cycle illustrated in Figure 2.1 in which inductive and deductive reasoning are seen as complementary, alternating components of the overall process of studying a phenomenon. Again, the distinction between experiments and case studies is blurred, with either approach being appropriate for either confirmatory or exploratory studies.

Thus the two prototypes of the quantitative (laboratory experiment) and qualitative (case study) approaches are not that different from one another in terms of the three dimensions that we have examined, provided that investigators are interested in causality. Yin (1994) recently came to the same conclusion when examining commonalities between qualitative and quantitative research. He listed four commonalities in examples of exemplary quantitative and qualitative studies: thorough coverage and investigation of all evidence, constant awareness and testing of rival hypotheses, results with significant implications, and investigatory expertise about the subject.

A TAXONOMY OF TRADITIONAL
DATA COLLECTION TECHNIQUES IN
THE BEHAVIORAL AND SOCIAL SCIENCES

A taxonomy of traditional behavioral and social science research designs is contained in Table 2.2. We have labeled this table a taxonomy of "data collection techniques" rather than research designs, a point that we will explain later in this section. Within this table, common types of designs are characterized in terms of the three dimensions of analysis presented above. Information in this table indicates that there are three general groups of traditional designs:

Table 2.2

A Taxonomy of Traditional Data Collection Techniques
in the Social and Behavioral Sciences

Data Collection Technique	Setting		Manipulation		Orientation	
	Controlled	Natural	Yes	No	Confirmatory	Exploratory
Lab experiment	X		X		X	
Single-subject study	X		X		X	
Field experiment		X	X		X	
Survey study		X		X	X	X
Relationship studies		X		X		X
Prediction studies		X		X	X	
Archival studies		X		X		X
Causal-comparative		X		X	X	X
Historical research		X		X	X	X
Case/field study		X		X	X	X
Descriptive research		X		X		X
Developmental research[*]	X	X		X		X

*Developmental research includes longitudinal, cross-sectional, shortened longitudinal, and similar research (see Salkind, 1997). Although these methods are classified as either descriptive or survey, we think they should be classified as a separate category because the investigators might use a combination of methods in such studies, from qualitative case studies to correlation/prediction and quasi experiments.

1. Group 1 controls settings and/or manipulates variables, with the objective of testing tentative predictions or hypotheses (confirmatory). Designs in this group include laboratory experiments, single-subject studies, and field experiments.

2. Group 2 neither controls settings nor manipulates variables, and may be confirmatory or exploratory. Designs in this group include surveys, correlational/archival studies, causal comparative studies, historical studies, and case studies.

3. Group 3 neither controls settings nor manipulates variables, and focuses on exploratory issues. Designs in this group include descriptive and ethnographic studies.

While this taxonomy has some interesting contrasts, it is unsatisfactory as an efficient way of classifying all of the different types of designs in the behavioral and social sciences. The first problem with this taxonomy concerns the number of designs, which in Table 2.2 is 12. Brewer and Hunter (1989) constructed a similar taxonomy with four types of designs. Yin's (1993) analysis included five types of designs. Research books from different fields have different elements in their taxonomies due to the idiosyncratic nature of the areas of study.

Second, this taxonomy is based on a set of three dichotomies that are a bit "fuzzy," as indicated by the discussion in the previous sections of this chapter. For instance, both the confirmatory and the exploratory dimensions are checked for 4 of the 12 research designs. Although distinctions between types of setting and the presence/absence of manipulations are clearer in Table 2.2, the discussion above indicates that experiments and descriptive case studies are more alike than indicated in the table. For example, confirmatory case studies have design characteristics intended to control certain extraneous factors in a natural setting.

A final problem with the taxonomy in Table 2.2 concerns the methodological "baggage" that the designs carry as they cross interdisciplinary lines. This "baggage" occurs due to different disciplines' preconceived notions about designs that have been around for decades. A good example would be case studies. Can case studies be confirmatory? Yin (1993), writing from an experimental psychology background, says yes. Many anthropological and educational ethnographers would say no.

We propose a more logical taxonomy for mixed model designs, based solely on the intrinsic characteristics of those designs, in Chapter 3. We have sought to avoid value-laden terms in this taxonomy of mixed model studies (see Table 3.1 in Chapter 3).

We have referred to the taxonomy in Table 2.2 as a set of *data collection* methods rather than *research designs* or research types, as they are called in other standard textbooks (e.g., Gall, Borg, & Gall, 1996). This change in nomenclature occurred for two reasons:

1. We prefer the nonoverlapping taxonomy of research designs (to be discussed in Chapter 3) to the traditional taxonomy found in Table 2.2, with its inherently overlapping categories and ambiguous cross-disciplinary distinctions.

2. The categories in Table 2.2 are, in fact, basically different approaches for gathering data. These approaches have emerged from all the social and behavioral sciences: laboratory experiments from psychology; single-subject designs from school and educational psychology and special education; field experiments from education and evaluation; surveys from sociology; correlational and archival studies from several fields including sociology; causal comparative (ex post facto) studies from evaluation, education, and sociology; historiography from history; case/field study and ethnographic studies from anthropology primarily, with contributions from sociology; and descriptive studies from virtually all the social and behavioral sciences.

These approaches represent the traditional normative methods for collecting data from these different disciplines. As such, they have been confused with research designs from those fields: experiments with psychological methods, surveys with sociological methods, ethnographic studies with anthropological methods, historiography with historical methods, causal-comparative studies with evaluation research, and so on.

In fact, there is no reason that sociologists (or any other group of scientists) shouldn't be able to use experiments, surveys, ethnographic studies, historiography, quasi experiments, and all of the other types of data collection methods while doing sociological studies (or other types of studies). Some of the most accomplished researchers have often used research designs not indigenous to their own discipline to answer their research questions. There will be more discussion of these specific data collection methods in Chapter 5.

NOTE

1. This methodology (Guba & Lincoln, 1994, p. 111) consists of (a) individual constructions being elicited and refined through interaction "between and among" researcher and respondents; (b) the interpretation of these constructions through hermeneutic techniques and dialogue among participants; and (c) the determination of a consensus construction. (According to Kneller, 1984, *hermeneutic philosophy* refers to the "philosophic study of understanding," which is "considered as interpretive" [p. 66]. Hermeneutics refers to the analysis of text, or literature.)

3

Research Design Issues for Mixed Method and Mixed Model Studies

This chapter presents a variety of methodological issues regarding mixed method and mixed model studies and a taxonomy of mixed model studies that serves as the organizational tool for the rest of the volume.

The Deficiencies of Monomethods: A Diversity of Imperfection

When pragmatists convincingly postulated the compatibility thesis, the link between paradigm and method was weakened, and there was a gradual acceptance among many behavioral and social scientists of the methodological orientations of others. During this process, critics of the incompatibility thesis spoke of the inadequacies of the monomethod designs. For instance, Brewer and Hunter (1989) described monomethod designs as "a diversity of imperfection" in the following quote:

> Social science methods should not be treated as mutually exclusive alternatives among which we must choose. . . . Our individual methods may be flawed, but fortunately the flaws are not identical. A diversity of imperfection allows us to combine methods . . . to compensate for their particular faults and imperfections. (pp. 16-17)

Similarly, Cook and Campbell (1979), in a discussion of the threats to the validity of research results, pointed out the shortcomings of monomethods in measuring underlying constructs. These influential quantitative methodologists described *monomethod bias* as one of the threats to the *construct validity of putative (i.e., reputed) causes and effects*. They contended that if a construct was measured using only one method, then it would be difficult to differentiate the construct from its particular monomethod operational definition. Using as an example the measurement of attitudes using paper-and-pencil responses only, they questioned "whether one can test if 'personal private attitude' has been measured alone as opposed to 'paper-and-pencil nonaccountable responses' " (Cook &

Campbell, 1979, p. 66). This criticism of monomethods was a follow-up to earlier work by Campbell and Fiske (1959), mentioned in Chapter 1, in which they asserted that there needed to be multiple quantitative methods for assessing psychological traits.

DESIGN ISSUES ASSOCIATED
WITH MIXED METHOD STUDIES

During the mixed method period (Period II in Table 1.1), there was a gradual development of a number of research designs that incorporated both the quantitative and the qualitative orientations. These approaches were developed in several fields, and they were to a large degree an outgrowth of the popularization of triangulation methods.

The Importance of the Concept of Triangulation

The concept of the "triangulation of methods" was the intellectual wedge that eventually broke the methodological hegemony of the monomethod purists. There were a series of steps in this process, including the following:

In 1959, Campbell and Fiske (writing in the experimental psychology literature) proposed their "multitrait-multimethod matrix," which used more than one quantitative method to measure a psychological trait. They did this to assure that the variance in their research was accounted for by the trait under study, not by the method that was employed (Brewer & Hunter, 1989; Creswell, 1995).

There was a distinction made in Table 1.1 between purely quantitative designs using a single data source and those employing multiple data sources. The work of Campbell and Fiske popularized the use of multiple quantitative techniques in the same study.

In 1978, Denzin applied the term *triangulation* in a book on sociological methods. The original term *triangulation* refers to a surveying/nautical process in which two points (and their angles) are used to determine the unknown distance to a third point. Denzin's concept of triangulation involved combining data sources to study the same social phenomenon. He discussed four basic types of triangulation: *data triangulation* (the use of a variety of data sources in a study), *investigator triangulation* (the use of several different researchers), *theory triangulation* (the use of multiple perspectives to interpret the results of a study), and *methodological triangulation* (the use of multiple methods to study a research problem).

In 1979, Jick (writing in the area of administration) discussed triangulation in terms of the weaknesses of one method being offset by the strengths of another. He also discussed *within methods triangulation* (such as multiple quantitative or multiple qualitative approaches) and *across methods triangulation* (involving both quantitative and qualitative approaches).

In an influential qualitative evaluation and research methods book, Patton (1990) described and gave examples of three triangulation methods: reconciling qualitative and quantitative data (across methods), comparing multiple qualitative data sources (within methods), and multiple perspectives from multiple observers (across different analysts of qualitative data).

Patton wrote extensively about triangulating multiple qualitative data sources while conducting evaluations of educational or social service programs. Often, this involved the use of both interviewing and observation techniques. The work of Patton and Jick has led to the popularization of the multiple use of qualitative techniques in the same study.

In a similar vein, sociologists Brewer and Hunter (1989) suggested that a multimethod approach to research is superior to monomethod research in that it provides grounds for data triangulation. Brewer and Hunter disfavored "composite" methods research composed of "elements borrowed from the basic styles" (p. 80). Although they acknowledged the strengths of composite methods, Brewer and Hunter stated that the basic methods lose some of their strengths when incorporated into competing methodologies. Also, they argued that this methodological eclecticism does not provide enough data for "cross-method comparison." According to these authors, triangulation of distinct methods provides greater opportunities for causal inference.

What Has Been Meant by the Term *Mixed Method Designs*?

As indicated in the previous section, authors from multiple fields initially defined mixed method designs under the general heading of method triangulation. As Creswell (1995) has recently noted, mixed method designs now serve purposes beyond triangulation (i.e., defined as the convergence of results). In an extensive literature review, Greene et al. (1989) defined five purposes for using mixed method designs and several design elements that were relevant to the choice of a particular design (see Box 3.1).

The complexity of making design choices in mixed method studies, noted by Greene et al. (1989), reflects the confusion currently surrounding

---

BOX 3.1
Five Purposes of Mixed Methods Studies

Greene et al. (1989) reviewed 57 mixed methods studies from the 1980s and listed five purposes for these studies: (a) *triangulation,* or seeking convergence of results; (b) *complementarity,* or examining overlapping and different facets of a phenomenon; (c) *initiation,* or discovering paradoxes, contradictions, fresh perspectives; (d) *development,* or using the methods sequentially, such that results from the first method inform the use of the second method; and (e) *expansion,* or mixed methods adding breadth and scope to a project. Greene et al. (1989) also listed design elements that influence the selection of a particular mixed method design. These design elements encompassed characteristics of methods, the phenomena under investigation, the paradigmatic framework, the relative status of the different methods, and criteria for implementation.

---

mixed method approaches. As noted in Chapter 1, Datta (1994) concluded that evaluators were using what she called "mixed-up models" because there was no consistent paradigm or theory for mixed method studies. Several authors have made attempts to create taxonomies of mixed method designs, including Creswell (1995), Greene et al. (1989), Morse (1991), and Patton (1990). An example from a multinational study of reproductive health (Ulin, Waszak, & Pfannenschmidt, 1996) is presented in Box 3.2.

We developed a taxonomy for organizing these different types of mixed method designs and presented it in Table 1.1. The remainder of this section will briefly describe each of the following mixed method designs:

- Equivalent status designs: Sequential (QUAN/QUAL and QUAL/QUAN) and Parallel/Simultaneous (QUAN + QUAL and QUAL + QUAN)
- Dominant-less dominant designs: Sequential (QUAN/qual and QUAL/quan) and Parallel/Simultaneous (QUAN + qual and QUAL + quan)
- Designs with multilevel use of approaches

It should be noted that the term *mixed methods* typically refers to both data collection techniques *and* analyses given that the type of data collected is so intertwined with the type of analysis that is used. We unlink data collection and data analysis in the next section of this chapter on mixed model studies.

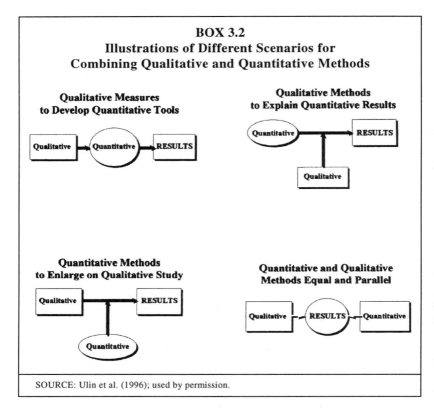

BOX 3.2
Illustrations of Different Scenarios for
Combining Qualitative and Quantitative Methods

Qualitative Measures
to Develop Quantitative Tools

Qualitative → Quantitative → RESULTS

Qualitative Methods
to Explain Quantitative Results

Quantitative → RESULTS ← Qualitative

Quantitative Methods
to Enlarge on Qualitative Study

Qualitative → RESULTS ← Quantitative

Quantitative and Qualitative
Methods Equal and Parallel

Qualitative -- RESULTS -- Quantitative

SOURCE: Ulin et al. (1996); used by permission.

Equal Status Mixed Method Designs

In *equal status mixed method designs,* an investigator conducts a study using both the quantitative and the qualitative approaches about equally to understand the phenomenon under study.

Morse (1991), writing within the field of nursing research, contended that the two paradigms cannot be weighted equally in a single study, but our experiences in educational research are different. See Box 3.3 for an example of this type of design.

Dominant–Less Dominant Mixed Method Designs

Morse (1991) gave several examples from nursing research of single studies in which one paradigm and its methods are dominant, while a small component of the overall study is drawn from an alternative design. These

BOX 3.3
An Example of Equal Status Mixed Method Designs

In a study of the marriage patterns in the Shona-speaking peoples of Zimbabwe, Meekers (1994) combined qualitative and quantitative methods of data collection and analysis. Qualitative data collection consisted of ethnographic research done by previous researchers to form definitions for the types of marital unions in this group. Quantitative data collection involved the use of an event-history survey suggested by Udry, Dole, and Gleiter (1992). A metal board containing strips representing events that occurred during the marital process was used in the survey. Respondents were asked to remove strips that they had not experienced, to arrange the remaining strips in the order of occurrence, and then to describe each occurrence. The descriptors were recorded on questionnaires.

Meekers combined the results from the ethnographies and the event-history survey by placing the respondents in the event-history survey in each of the categories found in the ethnographic findings. Three aspects were included in these classifications: the type of marital union, family involvement in the formation of the union, and family control over the couple's behaviors.

The types of unions were analyzed by looking at the percentages of each type within each educational level, area of residence, and age. The degree of family involvement consisted of the percentage of respondents in each of the types of unions who had experienced various events that would be considered to be family involvement. Family control was defined as the percentage of respondents whose onset of sexual intercourse occurred before each of the identified family involvement events. Meekers' results supported the ethnographic findings, indicating that young Shona couples have begun to deviate from the formalities of traditional marriage. However, her study found that the customs have not been totally disregarded. With regard to family control of the union, the study found that the family has little control over the onset of sexual intercourse and childbearing. The study did find that the family still has some control over cohabitation.

are known as *dominant–less dominant mixed method designs.* (See Box 3.4.)

It may be that in fields where one paradigm historically has been dominant (e.g., experimental psychology and quantitative methods, anthropology and qualitative methodology), the dominant–less dominant mixed method designs predominate. For instance, in experimental social-psychological research, an informal, often unstructured "postexperimental interview" is usually used to detect awareness of the main hypotheses and

---

BOX 3.4
An Example of a Dominant–Less Dominant Design

Creswell (1995) described a "classic example" of the dominant-less dominant design (QUAN + qual). In his example, an experiment (QUAN) is conducted in which a theory is tested and, during data collection, a short qualitative interview (qual) also occurs. While the information from the interview is useful, it is but a small component of the overall theory-driven experimental design. Creswell concluded that the advantage of this approach is that it "presents a consistent paradigm picture . . . and still gathers limited information to probe in detail one aspect of the study" (p. 177). Returning to the "bystander intervention" experimental study described in Box 2.3, if the researchers had conducted brief open-ended interviews with the subjects concerning their emotional response to the "lady in distress," then this would have been an example of a QUAN + qual study.

---

to collect data regarding subjective reactions to the study that might have affected the results. This component of these experimental studies are definitely "add-ons" that are in no way as important as the hypothetico-deductive-driven approach for the investigators.

Sequential Mixed Method Designs

In *sequential mixed method designs,* the researcher conducts a qualitative phase of a study and then a separate quantitative phase, or vice versa. Because the two phases are clearly distinct, this allows the investigator "to present thoroughly the paradigm assumptions behind each phase" (Creswell, 1995, p. 177). Creswell called this design a *two-phase design.* This design is popular with graduate students and novice researchers wishing to use both approaches in their work but not wanting to get into difficulties trying to use the two approaches simultaneously. In the QUAN/QUAL sequence, the investigator starts with a quantitative method and then proceeds with a follow-up qualitative study.

A dissertation completed by Freeman (reported in Freeman & Teddlie, 1996) is a typical example of a sequential mixed method study. Freeman first tested some a priori hypotheses regarding the differences in survey responses that principals in "improving" schools would give compared with principals in "stable" schools in a constant comparative design with numerical survey responses as the dependent variables. He then conducted eight case studies with principals in schools that had been identified as "improving" to try to ascertain consistent patterns in the processes whereby their schools become more effective over time.

In the QUAL/QUAN sequence, on the other hand, the investigator starts with qualitative data collection and analysis on a relatively unexplored topic, using the results to design a subsequent quantitative phase of the study. The Meekers (1994) study that was presented in Box 3.3 might be considered a partial example of this sequence (the QUAN was designed to clarify/replicate other investigators' QUAL). QUAL/QUAN is a common type of sequencing because in most quantitative survey research, the quantitative closed-ended instruments are developed after exploratory qualitative interviews have been analyzed or narrative data have been content analyzed. Carey (1993) presented an example of this type of sequencing (a study by Dressler, 1991). Due to the importance of Carey's comments on the study, we present his summary of the study in Box 3.5.

Of course, this process of sequencing qualitative/quantitative data collection or of using inductive/deductive logic is iterative and can go through several cycles, as described in Figure 2.1 (see Schuyten, 1995; Schuyten & Tashakkori, 1995). Also, other creative combinations of the two approaches are possible. For example, Floyd (1993) divided her sample into two. One group was studied with a QUAL/QUAN sequence. The other was studied with a QUAN/QUAL. Her study is summarized in Box 3.6. The two-phase design is the simplest of the sequential mixed method designs.

Parallel/Simultaneous Mixed Method Designs

In *parallel/simultaneous mixed method designs,* the quantitative and qualitative data are collected at the same time and analyzed in a complementary manner. While Creswell (1995) contends that quantitative results would not necessarily relate to or confirm qualitative results (and vice versa) in these designs, most studies using this approach generate numerical and narrative data that answer similar questions. For instance, a simple example involves asking teachers to complete a closed-ended survey concerning the degree to which their schools have been restructured, while at the same time interviewing their administrators about the same topic using an interview protocol with an open-ended format. As researchers analyze the numerical teacher data and the narrative administrator data, they would be looking for instances of agreement and disagreement between the two data sources regarding the extent to which the schools are perceived to be restructured. Box 3.7 contains an example of a parallel/

BOX 3.5
Carey's (1993) Summary of a
QUAL/QUAN Study by Dressler (1991)

Dressler's (1991) work provides a good example of how rigorous qualitative and quantitative health research methods can be combined. He was interested in the complex interrelationships between economic conditions, life-style, household demographic factors, and social support resources from family, friends, and the community as they affected the development of depression among African-Americans in a southern United States community. Dressler stated that he began data collection using open-ended ethnographic interviews (pp. 72-73). This generated information on community perceptions of stresses and other social conditions. Results from this phase were used to inform the construction of more structured and quantifiable survey instruments. After administering the quantitative surveys, he conducted a second round of qualitative data collection to obtain life histories and illustrative case studies useful for providing an interpretive context for the quantitative results. These different types of data allowed Dressler to construct a variety of quantitative scales, employ regression and correlation statistical methods, and provide as well a set of eight detailed illustrative case studies. All these methods and types of data were used in addressing Dressler's questions regarding the conditions affecting depression in a community.

He views the ethnographic case studies as a means to "simultaneously confirm what was observed in the statistical analysis of the survey data, suggest new avenues for investigation, and provide insight into the discourse of stress" among African-American community residents (p. 279).

SOURCE: Carey (1993).

---

simultaneous mixed method design conducted by Timberlake (1994) concerning homeless children.

Studies With Multilevel Use of Approaches

Multilevel research is common in both the quantitative and the qualitative traditions. These are studies in which data from more than one level of organizations or groups are used to reach more comprehensive inferences regarding behaviors and/or events. In educational research, for example, data that are collected at student level are linked to teacher attributes and school characteristics. Instead of "averaging" student-level

---

BOX 3.6
A Further Example of Sequential Mixed Designs

Floyd (1993) used both qualitative and quantitative methods to explore four questions: (a) Which sleep concerns were reported by adults? (b) Were these reported concerns related to age and gender? (c) Did the ordering of qualitative or quantitative methods affect the findings? (d) Did the two methods result in similar or different findings? Quota and purposeful sampling were used to create a sample containing men and women across three age categories. Qualitative data collection consisted of semi-structured interviews. Quantitative data collection consisted of the completion of a set of self-report questionnaires. One questionnaire, the "Sleep Bothers Questionnaire," developed by the investigator, provided two types of scores: a frequency of sleep concerns score and an intensity of sleep concerns score.

Within the age and gender groups, the subjects were randomly divided in half—one half to experience the qualitative interview first and the other half to experience the quantitative questionnaires first. Qualitative analysis involved Leininger's (1985) steps to thematic and pattern analysis. Four themes were found. Quantitative analyses involved statistical procedures, which included t-tests, ANOVA, and correlations. With regard to the first research question, the results showed that the sleep concerns of healthy older adults included health factors, changes in sleep patterns, and environmental factors. Qualitative analysis showed that the sleep concerns that were related to age were environmental factors and changes in sleep patterns, both of which decreased with age. The quantitative analysis did not show any concerns to be correlated with age. Both analyses indicated gender differences: Males and females were bothered by different aspects of sleep.

The sequence of the two methods affected the findings when the questionnaire was administered before the interview. The language used by the respondent in the interview was affected by the questionnaire. Some of the findings of the two methods were similar, but many were different. The combination of the two approaches identified questions and/or areas that need to be researched further that would not have been made evident by the use of just one method.

---

variables to obtain classroom-level data, both the student- and the classroom-level data are analyzed *simultaneously,* using complex models. A quantitative example of such research is the application of multilevel modeling (i.e., Hierarchical Linear Modeling or HLM) by Bryk and Raudenbush (1992).

BOX 3.7
An Example of a Parallel/
Simultaneous Mixed Design

Timberlake (1994) used both qualitative and quantitative approaches to data collection and analysis in a single study of homeless children. Conceptually, although the research was substantially grounded in previous theory regarding the role of self-concepts in coping (deductive), it was also open to the development of a new conceptualization (inductive) regarding the role of these constructs in the homeless children. A major objective of the study was to find the role of the "personal meaning of the homeless situation to each child."

Data were collected through interviews with homeless children and their mothers as well as questionnaires completed by their teachers. The teachers' questionnaire included a previously validated inventory (Psychological Functioning Inventory) used to measure children's adjustment.

Data analysis consisted of both qualitative and quantitative methods. Quantitative analysis included calculation of statistical indicators as well as tests of significance between well-adjusted and other children. Qualitative analyses included the development of a 3×2 grid based on children's meaning of homelessness. One dimension consisted of three levels of "substantive preoccupation" (separation/loss, caretaking/nurturance, and security/protection). The other dimension represented two levels of "action orientation" (passive complaints and restoration). Also, three modes of coping with homelessness were identified in the statements, each comprising several subcomponents. Successful and unsuccessful students, as classified on the basis of teacher responses, were compared on the number of coping descriptors.

Statistical comparison (t-test) revealed significant differences between the two groups. The article ends with detailed verbal descriptions of children's family, academic, and personal lives as well as a "profile of non-academically successful children."

It is also possible to do multilevel research in which data are collected quantitatively at one level and qualitatively at another. An example of such research would be conducting a survey of 1,400 students in three high schools while interviewing the three principals in detail and extensively observing the three schools for social-psychological dynamics. The school-level qualitative data can be used to make the student-level data more meaningful and understandable, and vice versa. Obviously, the two approaches can be used simultaneously or sequentially.

DESIGN ISSUES ASSOCIATED
WITH MIXED MODEL STUDIES

A major goal of this book is to present a different orientation toward combining the quantitative and qualitative approaches, which we call mixed model studies. These designs were briefly described in Table 1.1; the following section gives more detailed information on the taxonomy of these designs. Chapters 7 and 8 give extended examples of these mixed model designs, which involve mixing the quantitative and qualitative approaches in different phases of the research process.

The Overreliance on Method Alone:
Beyond Mixing at the Method Level Only

Throughout the history of science in the United States, there has been an emphasis on methodological considerations (e.g., Bannister, 1987; House, 1994; Ross, 1991). This methodological fixation was partially responsible for the paradigm wars and for their denouement through the use of mixed *methods* designs in the 1960s through the 1980s. House (1994) summarized this fixation with methodology as follows:

> Early in their development, the American social sciences shied away from certain issues of content because of strong political, social, and ideological pressures. Instead, they focused on methodology as a way to get to value-free, politics-free, and trouble-free findings that were consistent with an implacable belief in American exceptionality. . . . The position gave rise to a virulent scientism, a fixation on methods as the center of social research. . . . Overemphasis on method led to definition by opposition: If one method was quantitative, the other was qualitative; if one was objective, the other was subjective. (pp. 19-20)

When the paradigm wars, which were largely about methods, were resolved, it was perhaps inevitable that the resolution would also be primarily methodological. The new mixed method designs again focused on methodology, with less attention being given to other research stages, such as problem formulation and the inference processes associated with drawing conclusions from study results. While this was the case in general, a few authors (e.g., Brewer & Hunter, 1989; Creswell, 1995; Patton, 1990; Sechrest & Sidani, 1995) have discussed combining the two paradigms in several phases of the research process, not just the methodology. In their book on what they call "multimethod research," Brewer and Hunter discussed applying their multimethod approach to all stages of research, including the formulation of the problem, the building and testing of theory, sampling, measurement, data collection/analysis, and reporting.

Similarly, Creswell (1995) described "mixed-methodology designs" in which the investigator would mix aspects of the two paradigms at several stages of the research process. He discussed how this mixing might happen in writing an introduction, using literature and theory, writing a purpose statement and hypotheses or research questions, describing the methods, and describing the results. Creswell (1995) concluded,

> This approach adds complexity to a design and uses the advantages of both the qualitative and the quantitative paradigms. Moreover, the overall design perhaps best mirrors the research process of working back and forth between inductive and deductive models of thinking in a research study. (p. 178)

Thus mixing the QUAN and QUAL approaches throughout several phases of a study more accurately reflects the research cycle, which involves switching iteratively between deductive and inductive reasoning, as described in Figure 2.1.

Mixed Model Studies: An Alternative to Mixed Method Designs

As noted in Chapter 1, our use of the term *mixed "model" studies* indicates that these studies go beyond the mixing of methodology to include other stages of the research process. To mix methods only is too limiting; the qualitative-quantitative distinction cuts across more than "method." Also, careful reading of much of the recent literature in the social and behavioral sciences indicates that researchers are already mixing paradigms across several stages of their studies, even if there is no well-developed taxonomy for the types of designs that they are using.

The Patton Pure and Mixed Form Studies

In the following discussion of mixed model studies, we mix aspects of the qualitative and quantitative paradigms across three major stages of the research process. The mixing of paradigms across these three particular stages was first suggested by Patton (1990) in his discussion of what he called "mixed form" design. Our conceptualization of the three stages of the research process extends Patton's original model.

Patton (1990) referred to what he called "methodological mixes" using the following three components: (a) design (naturalistic inquiry or experimental), (b) measurement (qualitative data or quantitative data), (c) analysis (content or statistical). By combining these three dimensions, Patton generated six different ($2 \times 2 \times 2$) designs: a purely qualitative approach, a purely quantitative approach, and four "mixed form" variations. His conceptualization of these combinations is presented in Box 3.8.

Determination of the Three Dimensions for Classifying Mixed Model Studies

We like this approach of Patton's because it is very practical: First, how do I frame my research study and questions. Second, what kind of data do I collect. Third, how do I analyze and make sense of that data? These are the kinds of questions that we are asked most often in our methodology classes and in our consultation on dissertation committees.

We expand the three dimensions of Patton's as follows:

1. The Patton design dimension (naturalistic inquiry versus experimental design) is expanded to a "type of investigation" dimension (relabeled *exploratory investigations versus confirmatory investigations*). This alternative dimension is based on the distinction between studies with a priori hypotheses (confirmatory investigations) and those without a priori hypotheses (exploratory investigations).

As noted in a previous section, the distinction between natural settings and controlled settings is a continuum, not a dichotomy, in terms of issues such as the control of extraneous variables and error variance. The presence or absence of hypotheses is a dichotomous dimension that distinguishes between studies at different phases in the investigation of a phenomenon, with exploratory studies occurring before confirmatory studies.

This first dimension includes the formulation of the research question, or hypothesis. In exploratory investigations, the purpose of the study is typically stated in terms of research questions. In confirmatory investigations, there is at least one research hypothesis in which a prediction of results is made a priori.

2. The Patton measurement dimension (qualitative versus quantitative data collection) is expanded to include *qualitative data collection*

BOX 3.8

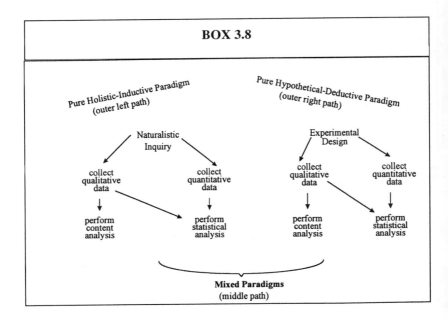

Pure Holistic-Inductive Paradigm
(outer left path)

Pure Hypothetical-Deductive Paradigm
(outer right path)

Naturalistic
Inquiry

Experimental
Design

collect
qualitative
data

collect
quantitative
data

collect
qualitative
data

collect
quantitative
data

perform
content
analysis

perform
statistical
analysis

perform
content
analysis

perform
statistical
analysis

Mixed Paradigms
(middle path)

and operations versus quantitative data collection and operations. This second dimension concerns the form of the data, and we think the narrative-number contrast is good for the purposes of an easily understood dichotomy (Miles & Huberman, 1994), although some authors have objected to its simplicity (e.g., Hammersley, 1992). (Chapter 6 contains an extended discussion of how narrative and numerical data can be converted into the other form.)

The relabeling of this dimension has been done for purposes of clarification: There are distinct research operations accompanying both quantitative and qualitative data collection. These include different measurement techniques, different methods for establishing the reliability and validity of results, different sampling procedures, and so on. These research operations will be discussed in Chapters 4 and 5.

3. The Patton analysis dimension (content versus statistical analysis) is expanded to include *qualitative analysis and inference versus statistical analysis and inference.* This third dimension is different from

Patton's dimension in two ways: Qualitative analysis has been substituted for content analysis, and inference processes have been added.

Qualitative analysis was substituted for *content* analysis because the former term is more inclusive and has been used in a variety of influential texts (e.g., Denzin & Lincoln, 1994; Miles & Huberman, 1994; Wolcott, 1994), while the latter is often identified with the field of communication (e.g., Berelson, 1952). Inference processes were added to this dimension because they are intertwined with analysis issues and because it was our intention to expand this taxonomy beyond methodological and analytical issues. An examination of the conclusion section of a published "quantitative" article or dissertation will show you that the authors make generalizations and interpretations beyond their obtained results. Each investigator has a choice of strictly staying within the limits of his or her findings or expanding the scope of conclusions through inference.

These three expanded dimensions are representative of the nine steps in the chain of reasoning for research described by Krathwohl (1993) and Gall et al. (1996).

The *exploratory investigations versus confirmatory investigations* dimension may include steps one through three: conclusions from previous research studies; explanation, rationale, theory, or point of view; and questions, hypotheses, predictions, models.

The *qualitative data collection and operations versus quantitative data collection and operations* dimension includes steps four and five: design or structure of the study and gathering the data.

The *qualitative analysis and inference versus statistical analysis and inference* dimension may include steps six through nine: summarizing the data, determining the significance of the results, conclusions, and beginning of the next study.

While the Krathwohl (1993) stages refer to quantitative research studies, the steps can, for the most part, also be applied to qualitative and mixed studies. Our intention in expanding these three dimensions beyond research methods (design, measurement, analysis) was to discuss the qualitative-quantitative dimension across other stages of the research process. The taxonomy based on these dimensions contains mixed model studies that go beyond the mixing of methodology to include other stages of the research process.

These three dimensions may also be referred to as stages of the research process: stage one, including the point of view of the investigators and the research questions or hypotheses; stage two, including design issues and data collection; and stage three, including data analysis and conclusions.

A Taxonomy of Mixed Model Studies
(Single Application Within Stage of Study)

We now present a logically exhaustive taxonomy of simple mixed model studies based upon the aforementioned three dichotomous dimensions, or stages. These simple designs involve single applications within a particular stage of research. These simple designs can be built upon to create more complex mixed model studies that will have multiple applications (quantitative and qualitative) within particular stages of the research process.

The classifications are based on the aforementioned three dimensions, or stages, of the research process: (a) the type of investigation *(exploratory or confirmatory investigation)* dimension, or stage, of the research process; (b) the type of data collection and operations *(qualitative or quantitative data collection and operations)* dimension, or stage, of the research process; and (c) the type of analysis and inference *(qualitative versus statistical analysis and inference)* dimension, or stage, of the research process.

A $2 \times 2 \times 2$ cross-classification of these dimensions leads to eight types of models for conducting research, which is similar to the Patton (1990) classification scheme for research designs. Similarly, two of the eight resulting types of studies are the traditional qualitative and traditional quantitative models. The other six categories are mixed model studies, combining components of the qualitative-quantitative distinction across different stages of the research process. (See Table 3.1 for an illustration of this classification scheme.)

These six mixed model studies are discussed in detail in Chapters 7 and 8:

1. Type I and Type II mixed model studies are confirmatory investigations (note Types I and II designs in Table 3.1).

2. Type III and Type IV mixed model studies are exploratory investigations (note Types III and IV designs in Table 3.1).

3. Rare mixed model studies (Type V and Type VI) are not very common because they involve the qualitative analysis of quantitative data. These mixed model studies will also be discussed in Chapters 7 and 8. Chapter 6 includes a description of *qualitizing,* or the conversion of quantitative data into qualitative data (or numbers into words).

4. Type VII and VIII mixed model studies are more complex types and are discussed in the final section of this chapter and also in Chapter 8.

Table 3.1

Classification of Methods According to the Three Dimensions of Confirmatory/Exploratory Investigation, Quantitative/Qualitative Operations, and Statistical/Qualitative Data Analysis and Inference

| *Confirmatory Investigation* | | | | *Exploratory Investigation* | | | |
| *Quantitative Data/Operations* | | *Qualitative Data/Operations* | | *Quantitative Data/Operations* | | *Qualitative Data/Operations* | |
Statistical Analysis & Inference	*Qualitative Analysis & Inference*	*Statistical Analysis & Inference*	*Qualitative Analysis & Inference*	*Statistical Analysis & Inference*	*Qualitative Analysis & Inference*	*Statistical Analysis & Inference*	*Qualitative Analysis & Inference*
Pure Quan	Mixed Type V (Rare)	Mixed Type I	Mixed Type II	Mixed Type III	Mixed Type VI (Rare)	Mixed Type IV	Pure Qual
Chapters 2, 7	Chapter 7	Chapter 7	Chapter 7	Chapter 7	Chapter 7	Chapter 7	Chapters 2, 7

NOTE: More complex combinations are also discussed in Chapter 8. They are divided into two categories: *parallel mixed model designs* (Type VII) and *sequential mixed model designs* (Type VIII).

57

Two General Types of Mixed Model Studies

As noted in Chapter 1, mixed model studies may be of two general types: those that have single applications of approaches, or those that have multiple applications of approaches, within stage of research. Designs with multiple applications are discussed in Chapter 8 and are divided into *parallel mixed model designs* (Type VII) and *sequential mixed model designs* (Type VIII).

These multiple applications are truly mixed studies because they include both the qualitative and the quantitative orientations within the planning of the study, within the data collection stage, or within the data analysis and inference processes. Examples include the following:

- You can mix both research hypotheses (indicating a confirmatory study) and very general research questions (indicating an exploratory study) when planning a research project.
- You can mix the collection of both qualitative (ethnographic interviews, nonstructured observations) and quantitative (structured interview protocols, observational rating scales) data sources when conducting a study.
- You can mix the analysis and interpretation of qualitative and quantitative data sources in an iterative fashion designed to expand the meaning of the numerical results using the narrative results, or vice versa.

Part II

Methods and Strategies
of Research

The following three chapters concern sampling and measurement issues, data collection strategies, and data analysis strategies. In these chapters, we present only a handful of unique mixed method or mixed model strategies because only a few exist per se. Mixed methods and mixed models borrow from both the QUAN and the QUAL perspectives with regard to methodological issues. Thus a researcher using mixed methods or models must be competent in both the QUAN and the QUAL traditions and must feel comfortable going back and forth between them. We have blended the QUAN and QUAL approaches somewhat differently in each of these chapters.

Chapter 4 concerns sampling, collection of data/information, as well as quality of collected information/data. Issues of reliability and validity of data/information are discussed, and a comparison is made between the QUAL and the QUAN approaches to assessing the quality of collected data/information. Chapter 4 also includes a discussion of issues pertaining to the validity and trustworthiness of *conclusions* and/or *inferences* that are derived on the basis of data/information. A comparison is made between QUAL and QUAN approaches to these design validity issues. An effort is made to distinguish between *design* validity ("inferences/conclusion quality") and the validity/reliability of *information/data* ("data/information quality").

Chapter 5 concerns data collection procedures. Each of the five basic data collections described (e.g., self-report techniques, questionnaires, observational methods, interaction analysis, and archival data/cultural artifacts) are used in different degrees by both QUANs and QUALs. Thus a continuum is discussed within the sections on these data collection strategies describing how QUALs and QUANs differentially use these strategies within their research. Again, the emphasis in this section is upon individuals who use mixed methods and models being competent and flexible in using these data collection techniques interchangeably.

Chapter 6 concerns data analysis techniques. Simplified matrices f both the traditional QUAL and QUAN analysis strategies are presente together with brief discussions of particular analyses within each traditio Chapter 6 also includes a few data analysis strategies that are ascrib uniquely to mixed methods or models. Three mixed strategies are presente (transforming one type of data to the other, construct identification/validatio analysis, and typology development). The emphasis in this chapter is on the researcher being comfortable and flexible in using the traditional approaches, plus understanding how these analytical techniques can be usefully combined in mixed strategies.

Sampling, Measurement, and Quality of Inferences

This chapter discusses different methodological issues in relation to collecting data for your research project. In a journal article, usually the second part of a research paper is titled "Methods" and presents the methodological information. In a dissertation, this information is usually (but not always) presented in Chapter 3. We will review in this chapter some of the issues, specifically regarding sampling and measurement, that you need to discuss in the "Methods" section of a research paper and/or project.

Components of the Methods Section

In the methods section of your research report, you present several important types of information regarding how your study was conducted. Usually, you need to include the following sections in one form or another: (a) sample or data sources, (b) variables and their measurement, (c) procedures, and (d) data analysis plan. Each of these sections is briefly summarized below:

(1) Sample/data sources. In this section, you define your unit of observation/analysis (who or what is being studied), how they are selected (sampling procedures), sample size (or number of units observed), and so on.

(2) Variables and their measurement. In this section, you first define your variables one by one and identify their possible relationship (e.g., dependent, independent, predictor, criterion). For research in which causal linkages are *not* of primary concern (such as in qualitative research, relationship studies, or descriptive research), terms such as *independent variable* or *dependent variable* are irrelevant and are not used. You then summarize how these variables are going to be documented, observed, or measured, followed by how you are going to

evaluate the quality of this information/data. We will discuss some of the available methods for determining data/information quality later in this chapter.

(3) Procedures. In this section, you present the details of your research method, design, and procedures for the study. If data collection and/or measurement procedures are presented in the previous sections, you do not repeat them in detail. All other procedures are discussed completely. For some QUAL research, the design of the study has emerged as the study progressed. This evolution is described in detail in the procedures section. Box 4.1 presents an example from a qualitatively oriented paper (Johnson & Pajares, 1996). Another example is also provided in conjunction with data analysis procedures in Box 4.2 (Chapter 5 contains more details regarding data collection procedures).

(4) Data analysis techniques. In this section, you present a summary of how you have analyzed your obtained information/data. Box 4.2 presents the data collection and analysis procedures of a qualitative research report (Jimenez, Garcia, & Pearson, 1995). As you can see, after reading these sections, the reader forms relatively clear ideas about how the data were collected and analyzed by the investigators.

Unlike the above example, in research *proposals* and in dissertations this section is usually long and very detailed. It includes the step-by-step "plans" for future analysis of the data after you collect them. For journal articles, because a major part of these analyses is presented in the next section ("Results" or "Results and Discussion"[1]), the data analysis plan section is usually brief and general. Chapter 6 contains more details regarding various data analysis strategies.

SAMPLING AND ITS LINK TO
GENERALIZABILITY/QUALITY OF INFERENCES

Sampling and the Generalizability
(External Validity, Transferability) of Results

Usually in either quantitatively or qualitatively oriented research, we are unable to study the totality of a population of individuals ("target population"). Even if the population is small, only a certain portion of it is

---

BOX 4.1
The Procedure Section of a Qualitatively Oriented
Investigation of "Shared Decision Making" (SDM)

Data were gathered from multiple sources, including regular observations, interviews, documents, and videotapes. Members of the research team visited the school several times each year during the 3 years of the study, observing Council meetings, committee meetings, department meetings, curriculum discussions, parent/faculty functions, and informal gatherings. Field notes were supplemented by videotapes of several meetings that were subsequently studied in depth. The nature of the field notes depended on the appropriateness of a particular method of gathering data to the observation or interview at hand: Some field notes were taken by hand during the contact; others were taped during private moments between contacts. SDM Council meetings were often videotaped by the media specialist, and, through this method, we were able to view and analyze meetings that we had been unable to attend. We sought to understand SDM from the viewpoints of its participants, and our largest source of data came from interviews. We conducted 167 on-site and telephone interviews with 92 individual faculty, staff, students, and parents. Of these, 156 were recorded on an audiocassette. Interviews ranged from 10 minutes to one hour and averaged 30 minutes. The interviews were semi-structured (see Spradley, 1980), and, although questions varied throughout the course of the study, participants were encouraged to talk about the SDM process at the school from their individual perspectives. All were transcribed into protocols. Field notes were taken to supply pertinent information about the circumstances of the interview not captured by the recording. Documents pertaining to the SDM process were also collected and analyzed—copies of minutes taken at all Council meetings, SDM procedural rules and guidelines, reports of the committees, and waiver requests submitted to the district and the state. We also obtained and reviewed brochures and pamphlets issued by the district on the SDM project.

SOURCE: Johnson and Pajares (1996, pp. 605-606).

---

typically accessible for a research project ("accessible population"). If you have some interest in making inferences and/or policy decisions that are applicable to other groups or to the population as a whole, you should try to study groups of individuals or events/situations that are the most *representative* of their respective "populations." Results obtained from representative samples of individuals or events/situations are more likely to be generalizable to the (accessible) population. The more representative your sample of individuals or events/situations is, the greater is the probability

BOX 4.2
An Example of the Data Collection and Analysis Procedures
From a Qualitatively Oriented Research Report

Data Collection Procedures

Group sessions. There were two stages to data collection. The first stage consisted of two group meetings where the Latino students in this study, as well as the Latino students in the large study, met with the primary investigator. During these two group meetings, which were conducted entirely in Spanish, students heard the purpose of the project, filled out background questionnaires, and completed measures of prior knowledge. The purpose of the second group meeting was to provide students with the opportunity to practice the think-aloud procedure. Students saw two videotapes. The first featured a Spanish monolingual child and the second an English monolingual child engaged in thinking aloud while *reading*. After discussing the videotapes, the students practiced thinking aloud with a partner. Students were encouraged several times to think about what they did while reading and to reflect on how bilingualism affected their reading. The primary investigator also met with the Anglo student separately and followed the same procedure used with the Latino students except that sessions were conducted in English.

Individual student sessions. The second stage of data collection consisted of individual sessions during which each student met with the primary investigator. For Catalina and Pamela, there were three meetings; for Michelle, who did not read in Spanish, there were two meetings. The students engaged in both prompted and unprompted think-alouds during these sessions. After they read each text, they were asked to retell it . . . Students were also interviewed during an individual session. During the interview, the bilingual students were encouraged to use whatever language felt most comfortable to them. Michelle was, of course, interviewed in English. The data collection procedures resulted in approximately 220 minutes of data per Latino student and 120 minutes for the Anglo student of interview, recall, and think-aloud data.

Analysis

Data from the prior knowledge assessment, interview protocols, and think-alouds were combined to create individual profiles of the three students. Qualitative research procedures involving coding, memo writing, thematic delineation, and presentation were employed . . . Before the profiles were created, the reading strategies utilized by the students during

(continued)

the think-alouds and mentioned by the students in the interviews were first identified . . . The transcripts for the three students, along with those of other students included in the larger study . . ., were read and reread by three researchers in order to create an emerging framework of reading strategies (e.g., representative strategies) that took into account negative and positive examples that fit or did not fit . . . Reading strategies were defined as any overt purposeful effort or activity used by the reader to make sense of the printed material with which he or she was interacting.

SOURCE: From Jimenez, Garcia, & Pearson (1995). Copyright © 1995 by the American Educational Research Association. Adapted by permission of the publisher.

that your research findings have "population external validity" (for a discussion of the link between sampling and the external/internal validity of conclusions, see Henry, 1990).

From the QUAN perspective, the issue of external validity of your findings is not limited to generalizability to the population of individuals. It also includes generalizability to situations other than the one you researched ("ecological validity"; see Gall et al., 1996) and definitions of each construct other than the ones used in your study. Also, when you measure a variable, you use a sample of items, a number of observations, or a specific way of measuring or documenting the attributes or events. These selected items, observations, or measures are actually "samples" of the possible population of ways of measuring or documenting those attributes and/or events. Hence external validity also pertains to the degree to which your obtained results can be generalized to other ways of measuring each construct. Overall, then, you can define *external validity* as "the approximate validity by which we can infer that the . . . relationship can be generalized across alternate types of persons, settings, times, and measures" (Rosnow & Rosenthal, 1996, pp. 158-159).

For most QUALs, generalizations to other individuals, settings, and times are not desired. For these researchers, the working hypotheses are only time- and context-bound (see Table 2.1). Generalizability of the conclusions/inferences of the study may be different to such qualitatively oriented researchers, at least on the surface. Some refer to *generalizability* as the "transferability of results." Others consider it an irrelevant concept. According to Lincoln and Guba (1985), *transferability* may be described as follows:

Naturalists make the opposite assumption: that at best only working hypotheses may be abstracted, the *transferability* of which is an empirical matter, depending on the degree of similarity between sending and receiving contexts. . . . That is to say, in order to be sure (within some confidence limit) of one's inferences, one will need to know about *both* sending and receiving contexts. We move then from a question of generalizability to a question of *transferability*. Transferability inferences cannot be made by an investigator who knows *only* the sending context. (p. 297)

Despite these distinctions, we believe that some degree of generalizability (whether labeled "external validity" or "transferability") of *conclusions/ inferences*[2] is important to all researchers. We researchers might need to generalize from a sample to a population, or from one setting to other similar settings, or to transfer conclusions/inferences from one context (specific setting) to another.

When you use mixed methods to examine a research question, you switch between different modes of generalizability. Sometimes you are more interested in generalization to a theoretical population, while at other times you might want to transfer/generalize the results/conclusions to another specific context. These differences in generalizability concerns are associated with the different kinds of logic described in the cycle of scientific methodology in Chapter 2 (Figure 2.1):

1. In the inductive mode, we are gathering data from specific instances to build up an abstraction or theory; the generalizations are initially from one specific setting to another (transferability) as grounded theory evolves, or from one way of defining/conceptualizing a construct to another (i.e., specific and concrete to general and abstract).

2. In the deductive mode, we are predicting outcomes that are supposed to occur in a theoretical population; the generalizations are from the specific sample that we are using for that theoretical population (population external validity). Or we might be making generalizations from one method of operationalization of the construct to another, from one method of measurement of the construct to another, or from one context/situation to another.

Babbie's (1992) discussion of sampling in field research (a title the sociologists usually use for qualitative/ethnographic studies) and content analysis might help you understand the link between sampling and generalizability/transferability of findings/conclusions. The following is a brief summary of his discussion:

Field researchers attempt to observe everything within their field of study; thus, in a sense, they do not sample at all. In reality, of course, it is impossible to observe everything. To the extent that field researchers observe a portion of what happens, then, what they observe is a de facto sample of all the possible observations that might have been made. If several people are shouting support for the speaker in a religious revival meeting, those shouts the researcher hears and understands represent a sample of all such shouts. Or if a researcher observes acts of violence during a riot, the observed acts are a sample of all such acts of violence. You will seldom be able to select a controlled sample of such observations, but you should bear in mind the general principles of representativeness and interpret your observations accordingly. (p. 292)

In content analysis of written prose, sampling may occur at any or all of the following levels: words, phrases, sentences, paragraphs, sections, chapters, books, writers, or the contexts relevant to the words. Other forms of communication may also be sampled at any of the conceptual levels appropriate to them. Any of the conventional sampling techniques . . . may be employed in content analysis. (p. 317)

The Internal Validity and the Credibility of Results

Traditionally, internal validity has been conceptualized as the degree to which we can *trust* the conclusions/inferences of the researcher regarding the "causal" relationship between variables/events. According to this conceptualization, your conclusions have internal validity if you are *confident* that changes in an outcome variable ("effect") can be attributed to a preceding variable ("causes") rather than to other potential causal factors (Cook & Campbell, 1979). As we discussed before, our conceptualization of internal validity is not limited to experimental studies and causal relationships. We, like a few other writers (e.g., Krathwohl, 1993, p. 271; McMillan & Schumacher, 1997, p. 183), believe that the issue of internal validity is very relevant to nonexperimental research and noncausal inferences such as those in relationship and prediction studies, in other descriptive research, and in qualitative/field studies. In Krathwohl's (1993) words: "Another view of internal validity is the power of a study to support an inference that certain variables in it are *linked* in a relationship" (p. 271, italics in the original).

This issue is specifically applicable to inferences about a relationship between variables on the basis of their covariation (i.e., when one is high, the other is high as well, and so on). Cook and Campbell (1979) have limited this type of internal validity to what they call "statistical conclusion validity" (p. 38). In their words,

It is useful to consider the particular reasons why we can draw false conclusions about covariation. We shall call these reasons (which are threats to valid inference-making) threats to *statistical conclusion validity,* for conclusions about covariation are made on the basis of statistical evidence. (p. 37, italics in the original)

McMillan (1996) presents another conceptualization of the issue:

Internal validity has already been introduced as a concept related to causal factors in an experiment. In qualitative research internal validity refers to a more general concept, the match between the researchers' categories and interpretations and what is actually true. That is do the meaning, categories, and interpretations of the researcher reflect reality? Is a pattern actual or have limitations in the data gathering or situation distorted the findings? (p. 251)

According to this broader conceptualization of internal validity, your conclusions regarding the *relationship* between variables or events have internal validity if you are *confident* that the obtained relationship (causal or otherwise) between variables is real, rather than spurious (as a result of other variables). As an example, assume that a researcher has found that male drivers have more accidents than female drivers. Although gender can't be considered the *cause* of car accidents, the issue of internal validity is very relevant to the researcher's conclusions. The observed relationship between gender and the number of accidents might be solely based on the sample of individuals, what is defined as "accident," and/or other reasons. If these alternative explanations exist, the conclusion is not internally valid.[3]

Such confidence is a direct result of your ability to "defend" your conclusions (to other experts, the reader of your research, and so on) by ruling out alternative explanations for your obtained relationships. We hope it is evident by now that a major assumption of such a defense is that there is a primary plausible explanation for a relationship or an effect, and that a certain degree of agreement between experts can be achieved regarding that explanation. In most QUAN research, this is dependent on your degree of actual or statistical control over extraneous variables (the *CON* in the *MAXMINCON* principle discussed in Chapter 3); in QUAL research, the confirmation of your conclusions by more than one method of analysis. As an example, McMillan (1996, p. 252) quotes Miller, Leinhardt, and Zigmond (1988): "Multiple data sources were used to compare the consistency of emerging trends . . . As often as possible, a trend that was identified in one data source was corroborated by at least one other data source . . . finally, the data were thoroughly searched for disconfirming evidence" (p. 271).

Internal validity is determined through a careful examination of the inferences that are drawn by the investigator. Krathwohl (1993) has summarized this process of evaluation in five judgments:

> The first of these, *explanation credibility* and *translation fidelity,* constitute the conceptual evidence linking the variables of a study. The next two, *demonstrated results* and *alternative explanations eliminated,* constitute the empirical evidence linking the variables. Finally, there is the judgement of whether there is a *credible result.* This last considers consistency with previous research and judgment of the strength of both the conceptual and empirical evidence. (p. 271, italics in the original)

To these, we would like to add the *inferential consistency audit.* This is the degree to which the inferences and interpretations are consistent with the analysis of obtained data/information and with other inferences/ conclusions made in the same study. A brief description of these six judgments/activities follows (see Krathwohl, 1993, pp. 271-280, for details of the first five):

1. *Explanation credibility* is the degree to which the explanations for the relationship between variables are theoretically and conceptually sound and acceptable.

2. *Translation fidelity* is the degree to which the conceptual framework of the study (questions, hypotheses, and so on) are translated into elements of the design, that is, appropriate sampling, measurement/observation, and other procedures. We discussed this as the "dictatorship of the question" in Chapter 2.

3. *Demonstrated results* involve the judgment of whether some results occurred and whether they were the ones expected.

4. *Rival explanations eliminated* concerns for the evaluation of the degree to which there are no other plausible explanations for the relationship. We discussed this in conjunction with *CON* in Kerlinger's *MAXMINCON* principle in Chapter 3.

5. *Credible results* involve evaluation of the degree of consistency of the results with previous findings in the literature. Under most conditions, theoretically unexpected results might create caution in accepting the inferences (question the internal validity). However, a strong study that meets other criteria mentioned above might be internally valid despite its

unexpected results *if* the inferences/conclusions follow the findings. As an example, methodologically sound *disconfirmatory* replication studies are valued by some professional journals. *Representative Research in Social Psychology* is entirely devoted to these studies.

6. *Inferential consistency audit* involves determining the degree to which the inferences and interpretations are consistent with the analysis of obtained data/information and also determining the degree to which different inferences and conclusions that are made in the same study do not contradict each other. This is highly similar to Lincoln and Guba's (1985) "confirmability audit" in QUAL research (to be discussed later in this chapter).

QUALs generally differ from QUANs on the issue of internal validity, at least on the surface, preferring to discuss the "credibility" of results. Some QUANs have also used "credibility" to discuss internal validity (for example, see Henry, 1990, p. 15). Also, as we discussed above, "credibility" has been considered *one* of the criteria for internal validity. There is a major difference between the QUALs and QUANs in their acceptance of who the "evaluator" of such credibility is. QUANs assess the degree of credibility of the results to others (e.g., to other experts). Most QUALs, however, assess the credibility of the conclusions by making sure that they are credible to those individuals whose multiple realities are reconstructed or described (Lincoln & Guba, 1985). In other words, QUALs determine credibility by how well they, as human data gathering instruments, represent the multiple constructions of reality given to them by their informants (e.g., Lincoln & Guba, 1985; Spradley, 1979). The degree to which these multiple realities are "defensible" to others (including the experts, or consumers of the results) is *not* an integral part of this conceptualization of internal validity.

As was the case with generalizability, you can see similarities between the conceptualizations of *internal validity* and the *credibility* of conclusions/inferences (to make researchers' lives a bit easier, we hope one day these two are integrated in a single term!). As we discussed above, a major difference between them is in the agent/person who evaluates the "credibility" of the *conclusions*. Please note that although information regarding behaviors and events might be available to the individuals who are studied, the *link* between variables and/or events is not always apparent to them (this is, indeed, a major assumption in many psychotherapies, marital therapies, conflict resolutions in personal and in institutional disputes, and so on). As we have discussed, internal validity is the credibility of the *inferences/conclusions* that are *derived* from linking these observations/

data. Hence considering the data source as the only, or even the best, evaluator of the degree of credibility of the inferences is not free of problems. Furthermore, much of QUAL research involves *content analysis* (discussed in Chapter 6). The QUAL-QUAN divergence of ideas regarding inference quality (internal validity) is smaller in such research. Finally, even when disagreement between the two approaches is indeed relevant, such disagreement is not a major issue for the mixed model researcher because he or she has the flexibility to evaluate the credibility of the results according to either or both criteria *as appropriate*.

Sampling and the Internal Validity of Results

The sampling of individuals or settings ("selection bias") might have consequences for the internal validity of research findings. For example, the relationship between two variables might be affected by the selectivity of the individuals who are observed (e.g., volunteer participants in a focus group or in a survey) rather than the other members of the same population (see Mangione, 1995, chap. 5, for examples in survey research). Some of the inferences made on the basis of the results might have low (or no) credibility. In experimental research, this is true if there are preexisting differences between the groups in aspects related to the independent variable (e.g., in quasi-experimental designs). In nonexperimental methods, this is true to the degree that the inferred relationship between two or more variables is a result of certain attributes of the sample under study.

These sample attributes are usually the result of sampling bias. An example of this is when a conclusion is made on the basis of a mail survey of teachers in a school system in which only unhappy teachers returned the questionnaires. For example, on the basis of such data, a researcher might conclude that there is no gender difference in teachers' job satisfaction. Lack of observed differences might be a direct result of the fact that in the sample of teachers who responded, teachers were generally unhappy, regardless of their gender (for a discussion of some of the issues in such mail surveys, see Mangione, 1995, chap. 6). Lack of observed difference might also be a result of poor "statistical conclusion validity" (see Cook & Campbell, 1979, pp. 39-50; Henry, 1990, p. 13).

Sampling Bias and Sampling Error

It should be clear by now that our confidence in generalization from samples to population is highly dependent on the degree of "representativeness" of those individuals or events/conditions. Before considering sample selection, we need to distinguish between "sampling error" and "sampling bias." Sampling error is random. Every time you select an individual, a text, a situation, or any "unit of observation," that unit of observation will be different from the population of such units. Hence you always have an error (we hope a small one) in generalizing to the population of units.

Usually, when you randomly select a relatively large number of units for observation/study, if some units are different from the "population of units" in one direction (e.g., if some people are economically disadvantaged), that difference is canceled by other units who are different from the population in the other direction. For example, if there are highly educated individuals in your sample, there are also individuals with low education. Hence the overall "picture" of the group will be relatively balanced.

To safely assume such balance through random selection of units, you must include a relatively large number of selections in your observation/study. Can you "randomly" select five high schools and assume that the students in your sample represent the "average" population (i.e., that the errors in sampling cancel each other out)? Can you select nine schools randomly, interview all teachers in those schools, and assume that you have a representative sample of teachers because the schools were selected randomly? Finally, can you observe three emergency rooms in an area of the country and make inferences about emergency rooms in general? We hope it is clear to you by now that the answer to *all* these questions is negative. For sampling errors to approach zero, you need to make a relatively large number of selections. If you can't select a relatively large number of units to study/observe, you will get more trustworthy and credible results if you select units on the basis of available information regarding their characteristics instead of on the basis of random selection.

The number of observations in your study might affect both the internal and the external validity of your findings. External validity is usually enhanced with a greater number of representative observations or cases. The term *representative* needs to be emphasized. Generalizability is not enhanced by adding individuals and/or observations that are not "typical" of the group of situations of importance to your research. Aside from the need for generalizability, in QUAN research, sample size affects the "statistical conclusion validity of the findings" by influencing the margin of error and the power of statistical tests to detect effects. We will discuss this issue further in Chapter 6 on data analysis. You may also consult Henry (1990, p. 13) for a discussion of the impact of sample size on the validity of the conclusions. For a guide to determining your sample size, consult Henry (1990, chap. 7) and McNamara (1994).

Unlike sampling error, "sampling bias" is systematic (nonrandom). For example, if for a focus group study you "randomly" select one of every five students who happen to be in the library on a Friday afternoon, you might have a biased sample that does not represent the views of "average" college students. This is true because students who are in the library on a Friday afternoon might be different from the rest of the population of students on campus. Unlike sampling error, increasing the size of the sample does *not* decrease the degree of bias in your sample. Obviously, the results of a biased sample cannot be considered to be representative of the population (i.e., the findings have low transferability or external validity).

Random and Nonrandom Samples

What should you do if your sampling unit consists of intact groups of individuals such as schools or clinics ("cluster sampling") and you can't select a large enough number of these units or clusters to have small sampling error? It is probably more advisable to select your units nonrandomly, based on information you already have about these units (see Maxwell, 1996, p. 71, for further discussion). We will discuss some of these "purposive" sampling strategies later in this chapter (also see Henry, 1990, pp. 23-25, regarding the "utility of nonprobability samples"). For example, if the racial/ethnic composition of schools in your sample is important to your research question, and you can only select three schools for your study, you might select schools such that your sample has the desired ethnic/racial diversity (one high-minority school, one low-minority school, and one balanced).

This type of sampling is specifically used in small-scale, in-depth research projects. It is, for example, widely used in qualitatively oriented studies that observe/study a small number of units. In Chapter 3, we discussed a study by Freeman and Teddlie (1996) in which a detailed example of such a small-scale study was presented from the school effectiveness research literature. In similar research, sample selection is performed on the basis of either qualitative or quantitative information that is available regarding the units of observation/study. A specific case of such information, for example, is when schools are selected for study based on an initial (regression) analysis of available archival data and are classified as effective or ineffective in an outlier design (e.g., Patton, 1990; Stringfield, 1994). We will discuss some of these initial presampling data analysis techniques in Chapter 6.

Types of Samples and Selection Procedures

Tables 4.1 and 4.2 present summaries of probability and purposive/ nonprobability sampling procedures. Although some of these procedures for sample selection are associated with either the QUAL or the QUAN approach, most can be used in both types of research (for an example of probability sampling in QUAL research, see Miles & Huberman, 1994). This is specifically true regarding the purposive sampling strategies in Table 4.2. These strategies have been widely used in descriptive QUAN research as well as in qualitative research.

Even within each tradition (QUAL or QUAN), sampling methods are often discussed as if they are mutually exclusive and as if only one sampling technique is used per study. This is, in fact, not true for many research studies in the social and behavioral sciences. You will typically use a combination of sampling techniques that are the most appropriate for your study. An example might be a "multistage cluster sample" in which intact units (clusters, such as school districts) are selected randomly, and then within each of these units, smaller members are selected randomly (see Henry, 1990, pp. 30-32, for more details). Your design might even require you to stratify your sample at one of these levels, leading to a combination of two types of sampling techniques (cluster and stratified).

There also are possibilities for mixing probability sampling with purposive sampling strategies similar to multistage samples (for a brief discussion of some of the complexities in such mixing in survey research, see Fowler, 1993, pp. 24-26). For example, you might select three schools in a purposive manner and randomly select students within each for interview or other measurement. As we discussed above, there is no single type of sample, or no sampling procedure, that is suitable for all research questions/ objectives. We believe that the distinction between sampling strategies should be made more on the basis of the nature of the question than on the basis of qualitative-quantitative approach. Obviously, as a mixed researcher, you have the option of mixing multiple sampling techniques.

MEASUREMENT QUALITY
AND INFERENCE QUALITY

One of the main concerns of the traditional QUAN researcher is to make sure that the data are collected in a valid and reliable manner. On the surface, these issues are not as important for the traditional QUAL

Table 4.1

Frequently Used Probability Sampling Strategies in Research

Type of Sample	Description and Sampling Procedure
Simple random sampling	Every individual in a population has an equal and independent chance of being selected for the study. The sample is obtained through selection by chance, a table of random numbers, or computer-generated random numbers.
Systematic random sampling	Based on the number needed in the sample, every nth person in the target population is selected for the sample. This method can be used only if a randomly ordered list of the population is available.
Stratified random sampling	This is used when the proportion of subgroups (strata) are known in the population; selection is random but from each of these strata.
Proportional	The proportion of each subgroup within the sample is the same as the proportion of each subgroup within the population.
Nonproportional	Regardless of the proportions in the population, the sample includes an equal number of individuals from each of the subgroups. The results are generalizable to the *subpopulations* rather than to population as a whole. This sampling strategy is useful for populations in which some minority groups do not have a large enough proportion that can be represented if simple random sampling is used.
Cluster random sampling	Already formed *groups* of individuals within the population are selected as sampling units. Because the group is the unit of selection, a relatively large number of *groups* must be selected. A sample of five randomly selected schools is not a true cluster random sample.
Multistage cluster sampling	This combines cluster sampling technique with others. For example, first select clusters such as school districts, then within each cluster select individuals/schools randomly or with certain attributes similar to stratified samples (see Fowler, 1993, pp. 18-26, for details and types).

NOTE: These sampling strategies are usable in qualitative research as well as quantitative ones. For further description of probability sampling techniques, see Henry (1990).

researcher because QUALs typically do not design elaborate instruments to measure their variables and themes in advance of conducting their research. Nevertheless, QUAL researchers do pay attention to the quality of the information that underlies their conclusions/inferences.

Unlike QUANs, the QUALs have combined the issues of information/ data quality (renamed trustworthiness and dependability) with those of design quality (the aforementioned external and internal validity). Some QUALs have reconceptualized these design validity issues as transferabil-

Table 4.2

Frequently Used Nonprobability or Purposive Sampling Strategies

Type of Sample	Description and Sampling Procedure
Purposive sampling	Selection of individuals/groups based on specific questions/ purposes of the research in lieu of random sampling and on the basis of information available about these individuals/ groups.
Sampling for homogeneity	Cases are selected such that they have the same quality and/ or magnitude of the attribute. Regardless of the size of the sample and depending on the objectives of the study, cases might be selected that are extreme or deviant/outliers, have a high intensity of an attribute, or are average/typical on an attribute.
Sampling for heterogeneity	Cases are selected such that their combination provides the maximum heterogeneity on certain attributes (e.g., ethnicity, education) that are important to the research objective of the study. Usually at least one case is selected from each level of the attribute.
Stratified nonrandom sampling	This is similar to stratified sampling but in a nonrandom purposive, convenient manner. Case or cases are selected nonrandomly (volunteer, available, and so on) from each subgroup of the population under study. In sociological research, this is also known as "quota sampling" (see Ary, Jacobs, & Razavieh, 1996).
Snowball or chain sampling	Select individuals on the basis of information obtained from other selected sample members or from other individuals. Because each new person has the potential to provide information regarding more than one other suitable case, the sample mushrooms as the study continues.
Sequential sampling	Start with a small sample and continue sampling until a desired level of certainty is achieved (see Krathwohl, 1993). In focus groups, for example, sampling stops when the new groups add little or no new ideas/themes to the ones already obtained in previous groups (saturation).
Convenience sampling	Sampling is done on the basis of availability and ease of data collection rather than in terms of suitability based on research objectives/questions. These samples also include what is known as "captive samples" (groups of individuals who are accessible to the investigator such as students in a class), "volunteer samples," "accidental samples," and so on.

NOTE: These sampling strategies are used by both qualitative *and* quantitative researchers. For further description of these and other nonprobability sampling techniques in quantitative research, see Henry (1990), and for qualitative research, see Patton (1990).

ity and credibility. As we discussed above, from the QUAN perspective, measurement validity is an attribute of the data/information that are collected during the course of research, while internal and external validity are attributes of the conclusions or inferences after all of these data/information are processed/analyzed. As such, internal/external validity is an attribute of the *end results* of research, while measurement validity/reliability is the attribute of the *process* (means) of reaching those end results.

QUALs have not made clear distinctions between these two components. A major reason for lack of differentiation between data/information quality and quality of inferences/conclusions in the qualitative tradition might be that in this research, data collection and data analysis are closely interwoven. A comparison of QUAN and QUAL research procedures will clarify this distinction. QUANs collect the data, evaluate its quality (validity and reliability), and then proceed to data analysis. Conclusions are made *after* these steps and are evaluated in terms of quality of inference (internal validity) and generalizability. QUALs, on the other hand, do their "data analysis" shortly after or while they are collecting the information, make inferences/conclusions, collect more information, "analyze" it, and make further inferences and proceed. Although in such research it is difficult to attempt a *separate* evaluation of data quality and inference quality, we believe that the criteria for evaluating these two are not necessarily the same. Hence these two aspects should be evaluated separately as much as possible.

In the rest of this chapter, we try to address the issues of information/data quality and inference/conclusion quality in three sections. First, we address the issues pertaining to measurement in general, especially in the traditional QUAN perspective. Then, we present issues of inference quality (internal/external validity) in general, and with specific reference to QUANs. Finally, we present the QUAL's conceptualization of these two components of research. As much as possible, we will try to differentiate the issues of quality of information from quality of inference in that presentation.

QUALITY OF INFORMATION/DATA: THE QUANTITATIVE PERSPECTIVE

Measurement, in a general sense, is the process of assigning labels or values to different levels, magnitudes, or qualitative aspects of an event or an attribute. Quantitative measurement usually involves assigning different numbers to differentiate different magnitudes of a variable. Qualitative measurement involves assigning labels and/or narrative descriptors to identify different groups of events, people, situations, and/or behaviors. By assigning qualitative labels/descriptors or quantitative levels (numbers) to different values of an event, we can differentiate those different values or levels and record them for later processing.

A great deal of controversy about "research methods" is, in reality, a debate over measurement methods. Investigators' tendency to remain faithful to one or the other of the two general approaches accounts for part of this controversy. For example, QUALs tend to avoid structured questionnaires and tests. QUANs, on the other hand, have often failed to take advantage of the rich data that are provided by unstructured interviews and the content analysis of observations and documents. Despite these separations, the basic principles and objectives of QUAN and QUAL approaches to measurement are quite similar. Perhaps the major difference is the fact that QUAN measurement is usually based on classification of events/attributes into previously established categories, while QUAL measurement is more frequently based on classification into emerging categories or explanations. Even this differentiation is not *always* true given that many QUANs might look for new categories or responses beyond the ones already predicted, and many QUALs use some preestablished criteria in their classification of themes.

Scales of Measurement

Depending on its nature, you may measure a variable on a variety of "scales." The simplest form of scale, known as the "nominal scale," is one that separates individuals and/or events into groups that are mutually exclusive. Examples of this scale are the differentiation of individuals according to their gender, ethnicity, and/or marital status. The nominal scale is a qualitative scale (differentiates qualities, not magnitudes). Hence, if numbers are assigned to differentiate the groups (e.g., 1 = male and 2 = female), these numbers are used as labels only and do not mean a better or worse standing.

In qualitative research, situations, events, and/or individuals are usually described in complex narrative forms that are, or strive to be, mutually exclusive (e.g., Lincoln & Guba, 1985). Although QUALS do not explicitly refer to these descriptions and/or documentation as measurement, they are forms of measurement. The scale for this type of measurement might be called a "qualitative-narrative scale." Instead of grouping events or individuals in qualitative categories such as in nominal scaling, they might be simultaneously categorized on multiple qualitative dimensions and described in narrative form.

When levels of a nominal scale can be ordered according to their magnitude and/or some qualitative attribute (e.g., attractiveness), the measurement scale is an "ordinal scale." An ordinal scale leads to a ranked categorization of events, situations, and/or individuals. Measurement of marital satisfaction, subjective well-being, and math ability are examples of such scales. A major problem with ordinal scales is that the same difference in ranks (e.g., $77 - 70 = 7$, as compared with $70 - 63 = 7$) does not mean the same difference in actual attribute.

An "interval scale" eliminates this problem by assigning numbers to levels/values such that equal differences in assigned numbers represent equal difference in the "true" attribute. For example, the difference in actual temperature between 85 and 80 is the same as the difference between 80 and 75. An interval scale has a zero point, but it is not "true zero." For example, a Fahrenheit temperature of 0 does not indicate that there is no heat. For this reason, if today is 80 degrees hot, and three months ago the temperature was 40, even though $80/40 = 2$, one cannot conclude that today is twice as hot as three months ago.

For such ratios to be meaningful, you need a "true zero." The measurement scale that makes this possible is a "ratio scale." Examples of such measurement are height and number of siblings. A person who has four siblings has twice as many siblings as the one who has two. Likewise, a person who runs four miles in a given period of time runs twice as fast as the person who runs two miles in the same time period. Unfortunately, very few educational, social, or behavioral measurements can be on this type of scale.

Scale of measurement has important implications for your data analysis as well as for the type of inference you can make on the basis of your measurement. Most commonly used statistical procedures assume an interval (or close to an interval) scale. Measurement of variables such as intelligence, depression, and quality of life (subjective well-being) are examples of ordinal scales that are usually interpreted "as if" they were interval.

Issues in Measurement: Validity and Reliability

Regardless of the nature, type, or scale of measurement, you must answer two basic questions pertaining to your collected data. The first question asks, "Am I truly measuring/recording what I intend to measure/record rather than something else?" This is a question of measurement validity. For example, let us assume that your research question involves "leadership style" among principals. You are administering a questionnaire to teachers to explore their perceptions regarding the leadership style of their principals. The validity question asks, "To what extent are the obtained scores for each principal true indicators of their leadership style rather than other constructs such as sociability and/or extroversion?" The same issue is relevant if you are observing a school to record indicators of the principal's "leadership style." Obviously, in both examples, before any answers can be sought, the theoretical meaning of the "construct" (leadership style) must be defined in clear form.

The second question is this: "Assuming that I am measuring/recording what is intended, is my measurement/recording without error?" This is a question of measurement reliability. If a measurement instrument is reliable, it should provide the same results consistently over time (test-retest reliability) across a range of items (internal consistency reliability) and/or across different raters/observers (interobserver or interrater reliability).

Much of the controversy regarding research findings lies in the researchers' inability to answer these two questions in an efficient and unambiguous manner. This is specifically true regarding measurement validity. Because most attributes in educational, social, and behavioral research are not directly observable (they are constructs, or latent variables; see DeVellis, 1991, p. 12), it is not possible to directly observe the degree of correspondence between a variable (such as creativity) and the obtained measure. How do you know if you are measuring "creativity" if you can't directly see a person's creativity? To make judgments regarding validity of measurement, you have to define the constructs in an observable (usually called "operationally defined") manner. A source of inconsistency between the findings of different researchers might be that they define the same construct differently. For example, some investigators have defined *self-concept* in a general form (e.g., as a positive or negative feeling toward self), or what has been termed *self-esteem* (Rosenberg, 1979). Others have defined it in terms of specific domains, such as self-beliefs regarding one's physical attractiveness or cognitive ability (see Marsh, 1994, for an example). Inconsistent results in comparisons of children from different racial/ethnic backgrounds might be attributable to these inconsistencies in the definition of the construct (see Tashakkori, 1993).

Determining the Validity of Your Measurement

Given that a construct is not directly observable, determining the validity of observations or the results of measurement (including the "human instrument" of qualitative research) is, at best, difficult. An instrument that "looks like" it measures political conservatism (or a qualitative/open interview to determine such an attribute in a person) might be measuring a range of attributes from need for approval to religiosity. Hence what the instrument (or interview) looks like ("face validity") is not really a good index of what it *truly* measures ("construct validity"). Face validity is *not* an indicator of the validity of an instrument. In fact, the less a research instrument manifests what it is intended to measure (the less "obtrusive" it is), the smaller the probability that respondents will react to their awareness of the researcher's objectives/questions ("participant reactivity").

Because the subjective judgment of respondents (face validity) is not actually an index of the validity of an instrument, you have to use other strategies to determine the validity of your measurement. There are two general strategies that you might follow. One is to ask "experts" to help you judge the degree to which a particular measurement instrument seems to measure what it is supposed to measure. Because experts do not agree with each other in many cases, this type of validation ("judgmental validity") is useful only for attributes that can be clearly defined and objectively evaluated. Another method for determining the validity of a measurement is to collect empirical data regarding the outcome of the measurement ("empirical validation").

Judgmental validation can be used for determining the validity of an instrument that measures a specific and well-defined attribute (such as academic ability or degree of learning). Usually these are based on a specific "content" area or a set of instructional objectives. Evaluating the degree to which a math test measures the students' mastery of course objectives is an example of this type of validation ("content validity"). Obviously, this type of validation is not suitable if the content of an attribute is not well defined. For example, what exactly is the content of attitude toward abortion or a political candidate? Although some authors *wrongly* refer to the content validity of attitude scales, or other similar measures, this type of validity is mostly applicable to measurement of academic ability.

Empirical validation is the most common way of evaluating the validity of measures. Usually, two types of information are *simultaneously* needed for this type of validation: (a) the degree to which the measurement outcome representing a construct is *related* to (consistent with) the measures of other constructs that are theoretically expected to be associated with it ("convergent validity"; see DeVellis, 1991, p. 50) and (b) the degree to which the measurement outcome is *unrelated* to (inconsistent with, uncorrelated to) measures of other constructs that are not expected to be related to the construct under measurement ("discriminant validity" or "divergent validity"; see Devellis, 1991, p. 50). Convergent validity also includes the consistency between the measurement outcome and the results of *other* measures of the *same* construct (in QUAL terms, the triangulation of multiple measurement methods). If the result of a measurement is valid, it should be consistent with measures of related constructs or other measures of the same construct *and* it should be unrelated to the measures of unrelated constructs.

The so-called known-group validation (see DeVellis, 1991, p. 47, for details) is an example of this simultaneous convergence and discrimination. Groups that are theoretically expected to be similar or different from others are compared with each other to determine the validity of the measures. For example, for a test of "creativity" to be valid, artists (who by definition are expected to have high creativity) should have a higher average score than another group (such as accountants, who might be expected to be lower on this construct).

Sometimes, in item analysis, if there are no suitable criteria to represent the construct, the total test score is used as a criterion for evaluating the degree of validity of each item of the test. If, in a group of respondents, an item score is consistent with the total test score (e.g., high "item-total correlation"), that item is considered to be a valid measure of the construct. This type of item validation alone is risky and should be combined with at least one other method. Table 4.3 contains a summary of different methods of validation in quantitative research. Note that although the usual techniques for determining the validity of measurements are usually discussed in relation to the QUAN approach, you can apply the basic principles to QUAL observations as well. The fact that a correlation coefficient can't be calculated for qualitative observations does not prevent you from evaluating the validity of your observations through other means, such as triangulation of multiple data sources.

Determining Measurement Reliability

Reliability is the degree to which the results of a measurement accurately represent the true "magnitude" or "quality" of a construct. Because we

Table 4.3
Methods of Determining Measurement Validity, Especially in QUAN Research

Type of Validity	Description and Procedure
Content validity	A group of judges ("experts") evaluate the degree to which items on a test measure the intended instructional objectives or the content (not useful for constructs that have no specific "content").
Concurrent validity	The instrument is administered to a group of individuals, along with an already validated (well-established) measure of the same construct. The new instrument is considered to be valid if the obtained scores have high correlation with the established test.
Predictive validity	A measure is considered to be a valid measure of the construct if it can "predict" a specific outcome of that construct.
Construct validity	This concerns the degree to which the test measures the construct. Because the construct can't be observed directly, a valid measure of *that* construct should meet *both* of the following conditions: (a) The measurement results should be strongly associated/correlated with other measures of the *same* construct or measures of those constructs that are theoretically related to it (*convergent validity*) and (b) the result of measurement should be unrelated/uncorrelated with measures of constructs that are *not* expected to be related to the construct of interest, or the test results should be different between groups who are known to have different degrees of the construct (*discriminant validity*).

can't directly see the construct, determining the degree of accuracy of the measurement outcome is not an easy task. However, there are indirect, and usually efficient, ways of determining the degree of accuracy (or the amount of error) in measurement of attributes. Two assumptions underlie most methods of evaluating the reliability. One is that if a measurement is accurate, it should be repeatable over time or obtainable with an identical method of measurement (e.g., a parallel test, a second observer). This is simply a type of triangulation of measurement simultaneously with two or more identical methods in the *same* group or situation, or with the *same* method on more than one occasion.

The second assumption is that if measurement has error (random error), these errors in representing the "true" magnitude or quality of the attribute will cancel each other out over repeated measurements. For example, if one observer has a tendency to rate an attribute more positively than it should be rated, another observer might have a slightly negative tendency when rating the same attribute of the same person. As the number of observations (or number of items on a test) increases, the errors in measurement of the "true" attribute approach zero. Table 4.4 summarizes different methods of evaluating the reliability of measurements/observations. Note again that although these techniques of determining the reliability of measurements/ observations are usually discussed in relation to the QUAN approach, the basic principles can also be applied to QUAL observations. We have pointed to some of these similarities in the table.

QUALITY OF INFERENCES/CONCLUSIONS: QUANTITATIVE PERSPECTIVE

Usually, at the end of the research process and on the basis of the collected and analyzed data/information, researchers derive conclusions/inferences regarding the relationship between variables/events. A major issue in making such inferences is the degree to which other, alternative explanations might be present for these relationships. We discussed this issue above in terms of the internal validity of inferences/ findings. Confidence in the correctness of the inferences (i.e., internal validity) depends upon the presence or absence of alternative explanations for the findings. We discussed a few of these threats to internal validity earlier.

For example, in the beginning of this chapter, we discussed the effects of selectivity on your confidence in the findings of your research. The relationship you have observed might be a result of the fact that a group of individuals/events that are being compared with others on a specific attribute (e.g., an independent or predictor variable) are also different in attributes other than that specific attribute. For example, after collecting detailed data, you might conclude that children with any pre-elementary school experiences have better IQs and educational achievement in elementary school (see Tashakkori, Haghighat, & Yousefi, 1990, for an example). This conclusion is reached after comparing these children with those who did not go to preschool or kindergarten before the first grade. As you might guess, these inferred differences might be a result of the fact that the children with such (preschool) experience come from different types of family backgrounds (in terms of socioeconomic status, social

Table 4.4

Methods of Determining Measurement Reliability,
Especially in QUAN Research

Type of Reliability	Description and Procedure
Test-retest	A test is reliable if the results of its repeated administration differentiate members of a group in a consistent manner. Usually evaluated through calculating the correlation coefficient between two administrations of the test in the *same* groups of individuals.
Split half	The degree to which results obtained from two halves of the test are consistent. Usually evaluated by calculating the correlation between the two half-test scores and correcting for length of the test (Spearman-Brown correction).
Parallel forms	The degree to which scores obtained from two parallel forms of the test are consistent with each other. Usually evaluated by calculating the correlation between the two test scores in a group of individuals.
Internal consistency	The degree to which items in a test measure the attribute in a consistent manner. Evaluated by calculating the (average) correlation between items in the test. Cronbach's coefficient alpha and Kuder-Richardson formulas 20 and 21 are examples of this type of reliability.
Interjudge or interobserver	The degree to which ratings of two or more raters, or observations of two or more observers, are consistent with each other. It can be determined by calculating the correlation between a set of ratings done by two raters rating an attribute in a group of individuals. For qualitative observations, it is determined by evaluating the degree of agreement of two observers observing the same phenomena in the same setting.
Intrajudge or intraobserver	The degree to which two or more ratings done by a single rater, or two observations done by the same observers, are consistent with each other. Consistency might be determined by calculating the correlation between the two sets of scores or through subjective comparison of the qualitative observations.

NOTE: For further discussion of these and other procedures for determining the reliability of measurements, see DeVellis (1991).

psychological attributes, and so on). Because there are other possible (alternative, competing) explanations for the results, concluding that pre-school experience is the cause of the differences has low (or no) credibility or internal validity. Of course, there are strategies for controlling, testing, or ruling out some of these alternative explanations. Some of these strategies are discussed below.

Some of the factors that might reduce the quality of your conclusions/ inferences (threats to internal validity) are discussed in Table 4.5 (also see Campbell & Stanley, 1966). In addition to selectivity, we have already discussed some of the threats to "statistical conclusion validity" as a result of small sample size as well as random variation (error) as a result of low reliability of measures (see Cook & Campbell, 1979, pp. 39-50, for others). Most threats to your conclusion quality are the result of lack of control over "extraneous variables" that might affect the variables of interest in your study. We discussed this issue in Chapter 3 (the *CON* in the *MAXMINCON* principle). For experimental studies, keeping all variables and events the same across experimental and comparison groups eliminates most of these threats. For nonexperimental studies, careful examination of possible explanations for your findings or other relationships between your variables, followed by evaluating and discussing the feasibility of such explanations, will improve the internal validity (credibility) of your inferences. Such evaluations are performed both theoretically (what is feasible on the basis of theory and previous research) and through reanalyzing the data to assess other possible relationships.

Strategies for reducing and/or dealing with possible threats to inference quality are presented below:

(1) Random assignment to groups. This is the most efficient method of creating two or more groups that are relatively similar in all aspects. Because the respondents are assigned to groups at random, no systematic differences in extraneous variables are expected between the groups. This is only applicable to experimental studies.

(2) Matching. If specific threatening variables are identified beforehand, the participants in a study may be matched on those attributes. Each of the paired individuals is then randomly assigned to an experimental group, leading to two highly similar groups on the matched variables. This method might be used in experimental research. In most of these applications, a sample is randomly selected; matched pairs (or triples) of subjects are formed and then are randomly assigned to groups. In causal-comparative and qualitative research, it is possible to *select* matched pairs of individuals and/or units of observation. For example, for each case in a qualitative study, a comparison case is found who is similar in certain attributes (e.g., gender, educational level).

Table 4.5

Some of the Threats to Inference Quality
(Internal Validity) of Research Findings

Threat	Description
History	Events during a study might affect one group but not another, leading to differences between groups that are not solely the result of the independent variables. In nonexperimental or qualitative studies, history might refer to events happening (to a group of individuals) over and above the event that the researcher is studying.
Selection	Certain attributes of one group are different from another group before the study starts. Hence differences after treatment (or a specific event in nonexperimental or qualitative research) are not solely attributable to the independent/criterion variable.
Statistical regression	When the subjects are selected on the basis of an extreme attribute (e.g., high or low performance), any difference between the pretest and the posttest might be a result of a (random) tendency toward less extreme scores. (If there is random variation, where can the scores of students with extreme low scores go?) The same threat applies to nonexperimental or qualitative studies of already established extreme cases/groups.
Maturation	Difference between the pre- and posttests might be the result of physical or psychological maturation of the participants rather than differences in the independent variable. Also, differences between two groups might be a result of one group changing (maturing) at a different pace than another (selection-maturation interaction).
Pretesting	Difference (or lack of difference) between pre- and post-tests might be a result of familiarity with the test (carryover effect) rather than differences in the independent variable.
Instrumentation	Differences between pre- and posttests might be the result of random variation (unreliability) of the measures (tests, observations) rather than the independent/criterion variable. Applicable to experimental and nonexperimental or qualitative research.
Subject attrition	Differences between the pre- and posttests (or between the scores of two groups) might be the result of the fact that individuals moved out of one group.
Implementation	The obtained relationship between variables might be a result of (a) experimenter/researcher/observer expectancy or (b) participant reactivity to being studied.

NOTE: See Ary et al. (1996) for details.

Obviously, in these applications, matched selection, rather than matched assignment, is used.

Randomized matching reduces the probability of differences between the groups on one or more extraneous variables. However, matching might also lead to subject loss (and weakening of the external validity) due to lack of matches for some subjects, especially when matching is done on more than one variable (e.g., education and income).

(3) Homogeneous grouping. If an extraneous variable (such as gender, ethnicity, education) is expected to distort the relationship between the main variables of the study, the sample might be divided on the basis of that attribute. Data analysis is then performed separately within each of these groups (e.g., within males, within females). For some QUAN studies, a more advanced method of analysis would be to use a *factorial design* in which the extraneous variable is considered a factor (an independent variable), just like the main independent variable of the study. This provides an opportunity to test the *interaction effects* of the extraneous *and* the independent variable on the dependent variable.

(4) Comparing individuals with themselves. When individual attributes are possible threats to the internal validity of the inferences, each person might be compared with him- or herself before and after a treatment. Some of the examples of this type of application in the research literature are the pretest-posttest, repeated measures, within-subjects, time-series, and single-subject designs. It is also applicable in qualitative studies before and after an intervention or event.

(5) Statistical control. In the absence of other possibilities for controlling the "effects" of extraneous variables, the last strategy might be the statistical removal of variation associated with these variables. Analysis of covariance (ANCOVA) is one of these strategies. It is used for comparing group means while controlling for the effects of an extraneous variable (covariate) on the dependent variable. Partial correlation is another strategy for calculating the correlation between two variables when a third (extraneous) variable is statistically controlled for (partialed out). There are also more complex statistical procedures (e.g., multiple regression, path analysis) to achieve this goal. Estimating the strength of the relationship, or the magnitude of the effect, *after* such controls is an important aspect of such applications (see Maruyama &

Deno, 1992, pp. 112-113, for a general discussion of magnitude versus statistical significance).

(6) Double blind procedures. These strategies are employed to deal with implementation threats ("researcher expectancy" and "participant reactivity"; see Table 4.5). To prevent participant reactivity, the participants are kept unaware of the exact nature of the study. To reduce researcher expectancy, the experimenter, interviewer, or observer is kept unaware of the main expectations or hypotheses of the study. Obviously, this is not possible if the researcher is also the implementer of the treatment, the observer, the data collector, or the person who does the content analysis of qualitative data/observations. For example, in comparing the relative efficiency of two methods of teaching reading, if the researcher is also the teacher, his or her expectations might affect the results. The same is true when teachers volunteer to use specific teaching methods based on their own preferences for these methods. Differences observed in students who are taught through these methods might be more the result of who the teacher is rather than the teaching method.

In the next section of this chapter, we will also review some parallel strategies for dealing with threats to the inference quality of QUAL research. Most of the strategies presented above are also applicable to QUAL research, and many of the strategies presented in the section on the qualitative approach can be used directly or with modification in other types of research. As a mixed method researcher, you will have the benefit of employing strategies from *either* group (or a combination of *both* groups) of strategies to improve the quality of your inferences/conclusions.

QUALITY OF DATA AND INFERENCES: QUALITATIVE PERSPECTIVE

As we discussed before, QUALS have not made a serious attempt to distinguish the issues of measurement quality (measurement validity and reliability) and inference quality (design validity, internal validity). Hence, in this section, we will discuss these two issues simultaneously, but we will try to highlight the strategies that are more relevant to determining inference quality.

"Trustworthiness" is a global QUAL concept introduced by Lincoln and Guba (1985) as a substitute, or analogue, for many of the QUAN design and measurement quality issues:

> The basic issue in relation to trustworthiness is simple: How can an inquirer persuade his or her audiences (including self) that the findings of an inquiry are worth paying attention to, worth taking account of? What arguments can be mounted, what criteria invoked, what questions asked, that would be persuasive on this issue? (p. 290)

Lincoln and Guba then introduced four criteria (credibility, transferability, dependability, confirmability) that collectively could be combined to determine the trustworthiness of an inquiry. The first seven activities listed below allow QUALs to establish the "credibility" of their findings. Credibility has been discussed at length by several theorists (e.g., Eisner, 1991; Janesick, 1994; Lincoln & Guba, 1985; Patton, 1990) and is the most important component in establishing the trustworthiness of the results and inferences from qualitative research. Different methods for determining the trustworthiness of qualitative research results are presented below:

(1) Prolonged engagement. It is important that investigators spend an adequate amount of time in the field to build trust, learn the "culture," and test for misinformation either from informants or from their own biases. As noted in Chapter 1, critics (e.g., Freeman, 1983; Gardner, 1993) have accused Margaret Mead of reporting misinformation given by her Samoan informants, partially because she had not spent sufficient time learning about the Samoan culture in general before focusing in on her particular area of interest. The purpose of prolonged engagement is to provide "scope" for researchers by making them aware of the multiple contextual factors and multiple perspectives of informants at work in any given social scene. Please note that this might be more relevant to the quality of information than the quality of the investigator's inferences/conclusions that are based on such information.

(2) Persistent observation. The purpose of persistent observation is to provide "depth" for researchers by helping them to identify the characteristics or aspects of the social scene that are the most relevant to the particular question being pursued. This activity might also be more relevant to the quality of information than the quality of inferences/conclusions.

(3) Use of triangulation techniques. These techniques have been described in Chapters 1 and 3 and include triangulation of sources (e.g., interviews and observations), of methods (e.g., quantitative and qualitative), and of investigators (Denzin, 1978; Patton, 1990).

As a caveat, it should be noted that many qualitative theorists and researchers do *not* triangulate because they do not believe that there is a single reality that can be triangulated. Denzin and Lincoln (1994) introduced the QUAL orientation of Richardson (1994) as that of a crystal, not a triangle:

> Traditional postpositivist research has relied upon triangulation, including the use of multiple methods, as a method of validation. This model implies a fixed point of reference that can be triangulated. Postmodernist, mixed-genre texts do not triangulate. The central image is the crystal. . . . Crystals are prisms that reflect and refract, creating ever-changing images and pictures of reality. Crystallization deconstructs the traditional idea of validity, for now there can be no single, or triangulated, truth. (Denzin & Lincoln, 1994, p. 482)

This, of course, is *not* the orientation taken in this volume, in which we promote the use of mixed methods to arrive at what may be called internally valid or trustworthy conclusions and inferences.

(4) Peer debriefing. This is a process of "exposing oneself to a disinterested peer in a manner paralleling an analytic session and for the purpose of exploring aspects of the inquiry that might otherwise remain only implicit within the inquirer's mind" (Lincoln & Guba, 1985, p. 308). This process contributes to the credibility of an inquiry by exposing the researcher to searching questions from the peer aimed at probing biases and clarifying interpretations. This is clearly relevant to the quality of researchers' inferences/conclusions following the data analysis. As such, it is closer to the idea of "internal validity" discussed above. So are the following two activities (5 and 6 below).

(5) Negative case analysis. This is a popular QUAL analysis technique (e.g., Glaser & Strauss, 1967; Kidder, 1981; Lincoln & Guba, 1985; Patton, 1990; Yin, 1994) that may be described as follows: "Where patterns and trends have been identified, our understanding of those patterns and trends is increased by considering the instances and cases that do not fit within the pattern" (Patton, 1990, p. 328). Negative

case analysis aims to eliminate instances that do not fit the pattern by revising that pattern until the instance also fits.

(6) Referential adequacy. This technique involves storing in archives some part of the raw qualitative data for later recall and reanalysis purposes (e.g., Eisner, 1975, 1991; Lincoln & Guba, 1985). Originally proposed for use with videotape recordings and cinematography, the idea has been extended to all forms of qualitative data. Reanalysis may be done by the original investigator or other analysts, and new interpretations can be checked against the original interpretations for credibility purposes.

A direct analogy can be drawn between referential adequacy and statistical analysis. For instance, researchers using regression analysis sometimes split their sample, running the analysis on the first half for exploratory purposes and then on the second half for confirmatory purposes. Again, the underlying logic of the QUAL or QUAN analysis is the same; one uses text of some sort (e.g., words, pictures) while the other uses numbers.

(7) Member checks. This occurs either during the investigation or at its conclusion, and constitutes the most important credibility check. Several authors have described this process (e.g., Lincoln & Guba, 1985; Spradley, 1979), which involves asking members of the social scene to check the analytic categories, conclusions, and interpretations of the investigators. Spradley (1979) advocated the use of structural questions, which asked informants to confirm the analytic domains that the investigators had constructed. If the informants or audience members agree with the interpretations of the investigators, then this provides evidence for the credibility of the results.

(8) Thick description. This technique provides evidence for the transferability of interpretations and conclusions from QUAL investigations. As noted above, QUALs are interested in the transferring of inferences from a specific sending context to a specific receiving context, and this necessarily involves the detailed description of all information (i.e., thick descriptions) concerning the sending context (Geertz, 1973; Lincoln & Guba, 1985). This is close to the idea of "external" validity of inferences/conclusions in general and specifically in QUAN research.

(9) Dependability audit. Lincoln and Guba (1985) concluded that the dependability audit concerns the *process* of the inquiry, including the

appropriateness of inquiry decisions and methodological shifts. This activity can be incorporated into the more general notion of "translation fidelity" discussed above (Krathwohl, 1993).

(10) Confirmability audit. Lincoln and Guba (1985) concluded that the confirmability audit concerns the *product* of the inquiry (i.e., attesting that the findings and interpretations are supported by the data and are internally coherent). We called this process the "inferential consistency audit"—an activity for determining the internal validity of inferences.

(11) Reflexive journal. This technique provides information for all four criteria of trustworthiness (i.e., credibility, transferability, dependability, and confirmability). Lincoln and Guba (1985) describe the reflexive journal as

> a kind of diary in which the investigator on a daily basis, or as needed, records a variety of information about *self . . .* and *method.* With respect to the self, the reflexive journal might be thought of as providing the same kind of data about the *human* instrument that is often provided about the paper-and pencil or brass instruments used in conventional studies. With respect to method, the journal provides information about methodological decisions made and the reasons for making them—information also of great import for the auditor. (p. 327, italics in the original)

Our final conclusion for this chapter is that although the types of "activities" for determining the "credibility" of QUAL inferences and the "internal validity" of QUAN inferences are not necessarily the same, the two approaches to defining the "quality of inferences" as a result of observations/data are highly similar. As such, a merged framework that includes elements of both approaches is very feasible and within reach. We have tried to point to these commonalities and similarities in this chapter, and we hope we can create a *superordinate framework for evaluating the quality of research findings/inferences* in the future.

NOTES

1. We favor a combined section titled "Results and Discussion" followed by a "Conclusion" section. Having a combined "Results and Discussion" section provides a more dynamic way of presenting the data, questioning each aspect of it (e.g., other possible ways of interpreting it, threats to validity), and following these questions with new

analyses. Presenting the results in one section, and then discussing them in a separate section, is less dynamic.

2. External validity pertains to conclusions drawn during or after analysis. These conclusions and inferences are made regarding the *relationship* between variables and/or events. Although the quality of information or data influences the external validity of these conclusions, it should be distinguished from it. Quality (validity and reliability) of data/information should be evaluated *before* inferences/conclusions are made regarding the relationship between these variables.

3. Another example is the inferred relationship between the age of death and gender in a "prediction study." Gender is not the cause of death. However, if this conclusion is internally valid (if the relationship is not a result of chance, bad measurement, an inappropriate population, or the like), a life insurance company can use gender to "predict" the age of death. If you were in a decision-making position in a life insurance company, would you use gender to predict the age of death if you were not confident that the obtained relationship was indeed trustworthy (internally valid)?

5

Data Collection Strategies and Research Procedures

TRADITIONAL AND ALTERNATIVE APPROACHES TO DATA COLLECTION

A noticeable attribute of the traditional approach to data collection is the researcher's "faithfulness" to either the qualitative or the quantitative tradition. Despite this faithfulness, an increasing number of researchers are collecting both quantitative and qualitative data in a single study. Researchers from different disciplines have advocated this "multiple" approach to data collection. For example, Sechrest and Sidani (1995) suggest that in each of the four stages of research (data collection, data analysis, interpretation, and use), two approaches are possible: "formulaic" and "clinical." Their "formulaic" data collection consists of traditionally focused/structured measurement procedures such as questionnaires, structured interviews, and observation protocols. Clinical data collection mainly consists of clinical interviews, unstructured observations, and overall evaluations of documents.

These data collection methods often provide new and uncharted information about the person or the setting of study. Each of these approaches to data collection alone might provide insufficient and/or partially incorrect data. Combining the two approaches (what Sechrest and Sidani call multiple measures or complementary measures) provides richer data than either approach. The alternative approach either validates the data collected through the other approach or complements (adds to) such data.

Complementary measures, or what we call mixed measures, might be used in the same measurement format. For example, in a "funnel interview," you might ask broad and open-ended questions to solicit unrestricted information from the respondents, followed by several closed-ended or structured questions that have a preplanned response format. In a more commonly used approach, you might have predetermined response options for questions, followed by an "other" response option with a blank space. The respondents are encouraged to write additional comments or provide additional data by writing them in that space. In the next chapter, we discuss the possibilities for analysis procedures on these "mixed" or "complementary" data.

Although most research textbooks distinguish between qualitative and quantitative data collection procedures, we do not present them in such a format for at least three reasons: (a) Most data collection procedures (e.g., interviews) can use *both* data collection approaches in one study/setting; (b) almost all data collection formats can benefit from a mixed or complementary approach; and (c) even the traditional data collection formats can be placed on a continuum from highly structured/quantitative to highly informal/qualitative. Instead of discussing different data collection procedures in each of the two traditional approaches, we discuss each of the main data collection procedures or formats separately and point to the possibility of collecting complementary or mixed method data within that format. For example, in presentation of the personal interview as a data collection format, we will discuss both the open-ended (qualitative) and the structured or closed-ended (quantitative) aspects of it.

Data Collection as a Planned Strategy

The traditional quantitative approach to data collection involves relatively detailed and planned "instruments" for data collection. On the other hand, most traditional qualitative research has been conducted without such preplanned methods of data collection for measurement/observation. However, most qualitative researchers have at least a set of strategies regarding the type of data collection method to use (i.e., observation, interview, and so on) or even the type of behaviors and/or descriptors on which to focus. In Miles and Huberman's (1994) words:

> Knowing what you want to find out, at least initially, leads inexorably to the question of how you will get that information. . . . If I want to find out how suspects are arrested and booked, I may decide to *interview* people associated with this activity (police officers, suspects, attorneys), *observe* bookings, and collect arrest-relevant *documents* (e.g., regulations, transcripts) . . . Even when the instrumentation is an open-ended interview or observation, some technical choices must be made: Will notes be taken? Of what sort? Will the transaction be tape-recorded? Listened to afterwards? Transcribed? How will notes be written up? (p. 35)

In essence, then, data collection in both traditional approaches might be identified on a continuum of unplanned to highly planned. On one side of that continuum are data collection efforts that are accidental or are without *any* previous ideas about *what* to observe or collect data on, and *how* to do it. It is difficult to imagine such a completely unplanned observation or data collection strategy in research. Most "unplanned" data collection efforts are planned at least in *some aspects*. On the other side of the continuum, there are highly structured measurements such as personality questionnaires and attitude scales discussed in later parts of this chapter. Miles and Huberman (1994) review the arguments for and against having planned measurement/instrumentation. Box 5.1 summarizes these arguments.

We believe that data collection should be as planned as possible, given the research question. For some research questions, only a limited amount of preparation is possible. For most others, there is usually enough prior knowledge to enable you to form more planned strategies. Regardless of the degree of preparation that is possible or desirable, a mixed model data collection approach gives you the advantage of using both strategies

Effects of Data Collection on the Behavior or Responses of the Participants

A major difficulty in data collection pertains to individuals' awareness of being studied (participant reactivity). People react to this awareness in a variety of ways that can affect the accuracy of the data and the internal validity or trustworthiness of the findings (see Rosnow & Rosenthal, 1996, for more detail). Similar to other social interaction situations, people who participate in a research study take specific roles. An individual might take a variety of "roles" in reaction to his or her awareness of being a participant in research. Some of these possible roles are (a) "good" or "helpful" participant, (b) "apprehensive" participant, (c) "faithful" or "honest" participant, (d) "suspicious" participant, and/or (e) "antagonistic" participant. A brief description of each of these participant roles is presented in Box 5.2. Although most research textbooks discuss these participant roles in relation to experimental methods, they are also applicable to all other types of research.

Determining what exact role a participant in research has taken is usually impossible. Obviously, you want the participants in your research to respond as honestly as possible and/or to behave in as natural and an uncontrolled manner as they do when they are not being observed/studied. Providing information regarding the importance of your research, appealing to the participants' sense of altruism, and creating a sense of professional trust will reduce the probability of intentional misinformation and/or

BOX 5.1
Miles and Huberman's Summary of Arguments For
and Against Planned Instrumentation in Qualitative Research

Arguments for Little Prior Instrumentation

1. Predesigned and structured instruments blind the researcher to the site. If the most important phenomena or underlying constructs at work in the field are not in the instruments, they will be overlooked or misrepresented.

2. Prior instrumentation is usually context-stripped; it lusts for universality, uniformity, and comparability. But qualitative research lives and breathes through seeing the context; it is the particularities that produce the generalities, not the reverse.

3. Many qualitative studies involve single cases, with few people involved. Who needs questionnaires, observation schedules, or tests whose usual function is to yield economical, comparable, and parametric distributions for large samples?

4. The lion's share of fieldwork consists of taking notes, recording events (conversations, meetings), and picking up things (documents, products, artifacts). *Instrumentation* is a misnomer. Some orienting questions, some headings for observations, and a rough and ready document analysis form are all you need at the start—perhaps all you will ever need in the course of the study.

Arguments for a Lot of Prior Instrumentation

1. If you know what you are after, there is no reason not to plan in advance how to collect the information.

2. If interview schedules or observation schedules are not focused, too much superfluous information will be collected. An overload of data will compromise the efficiency and power of the analysis.

3. Using the same instruments as in prior studies is the only way we can converse across studies. Otherwise the work will be non-comparable, except in a very global way. We need common instruments to build theory, to improve explanations or predictions, and to make recommendations about practice.

4. A biased or uninformed researcher will ask partial questions, take selective notes, make unreliable observations, and skew information. The data will be invalid and unreliable. Using validated instruments well is the best guarantee of dependable and meaningful findings.

SOURCE: From Miles and Huberman (1994, p. 34).

BOX 5.2
Some Possible Roles the Participants of a
Research Study Might Take During the Investigation

"Good" participant: A participant who tries to "help" the investigator by behaving in accordance with what he or she thinks the researcher is expecting. This type of participant attempts to help the investigator support the hypotheses and/or the predictions.

"Apprehensive" participant: This type of participant is concerned about the investigator's perception of him or her. To prevent an undesirable impression, the responses and/or behaviors are manipulated. This type of participant is more apt to act in a socially desirable manner.

"Suspicious" participant: This type of participant does not trust the stated purpose of the study or the investigator's objectives. Hence he or she behaves in a manner irrelevant to the instructions.

"Negativistic" participant: Similar to the suspicious participant, this type of participant is suspicious of the investigator and/or the objective of the study. In response to such suspicions, or due to other reasons, the participant acts in a manner opposite to what he or she thinks the investigator is predicting.

"Faithful" participant: This is the ideal participant in a study. This type of participant tries to respond and/or behave in a "real" and "true" manner, regardless of his or her perceptions of the investigator and/or predictions/expectations of the study. The participant, in essence, remains faithful to the truth rather than to his or her perceptions of the investigation.

---

controlled behavior. However, these strategies do not eliminate the possibility of unintentional reactions of the participants in your research. Post-data collection (or postexperimental) interviews with the participants in your study are usually possible and provide information regarding possible effects of these roles. You may ask all or a sample of participants/respondents about their feelings, thoughts, and attitudes concerning your study and their participation in it. You should also ask questions regarding the participants' "guesses" about the main objectives of the study and the extent to which these guesses might have affected their behaviors/reactions.

A comforting issue concerning these reactions is that in well-conducted research, the participants rarely develop a "uniform" view of the purposes and expectations of the research or researcher. Therefore, a uniform reaction (bias) is not present. Also, most social science research is multifaceted and involves a web of relationships between a variety of variables. It is very unlikely that a participant in such research gains awareness of expectancies, predictions, or even the main objectives of the study.

Obviously, these are all dependent on the degree to which you, as a researcher, refrain from conveying the main objectives of your research.[1] In behavioral or educational experiments, reducing awareness of research expectations and objectives by providing convincing but wrong information regarding them is often necessary. This necessary "deception" is not limited to experiments. However, information about the "true" objectives should be conveyed to the participants as soon as possible after the data are collected (see Greenberg & Folger, 1988, for a discussion of issues surrounding "deception").

DATA COLLECTION STRATEGIES

Generally speaking, you can use several methods (or formats) for collecting data. Although asking people about the issues/attributes related to them or others is the most widely used format for data collection, it has its disadvantages. Other data collection procedures attempt to collect information about individual behaviors and attributes through behavioral observations and analysis of artifacts and products created by the individuals. In addition to these, you might use the information already collected by other people/agencies (such as schools) or created by individuals (e.g., diaries) in your research. We will review the following general categories of procedures:

1. Asking individuals for information and/or experiences
2. Seeing what people do, recording what they do, or making inferences
3. Asking individuals about their relationship with others
4. Using data collected and/or documented by others

Asking Individuals for Information and/or Experiences: Self-Report Techniques

Self-reports are the most frequent sources of data in traditional quantitative and qualitative research. These are measures in which individuals are asked to report on their feelings, beliefs, attitudes, and other attributes. Most of our stated problems regarding "reactivity" might apply to these methods of data collection. Also, you should be aware of "response sets" (the tendency to respond in a certain manner). Some of these response set biases are *acquiescence bias/agreement* ("yea-saying" or the tendency to agree), *extremity bias* (the tendency to pick the end points of a response scale), *central tendency bias* (the tendency to select the middle of the response scale, the tendency to be "average"), and *positivity bias* (selecting the positive side of the response option). These biases are especially damaging if a specific group of respondents has a bias tendency while others do not. Differences observed between the groups may be the result of these differential response tendencies rather than any "real" dissimilarities. Any inferences/conclusions made on the basis of these results will have low internal validity (inference quality or trustworthiness). As an example, see Marin and Marin (1991, chap. 6) for a discussion of such tendencies among Hispanics. For further discussion of these and other response tendencies in general, see Mangione (1995, pp. 33-36).

Interview. The interview is more frequently used as a method of data collection in qualitative research than in quantitative research. Although textbooks classify interviews into qualitative and quantitative, there actually is a continuum ranging from unstructured and open-ended to highly structured and closed-ended. The traditional qualitative interview is located on one side of the continuum while the traditional "quantitative" interview is on the other side. The qualitative interview is usually nondirective and very general ("Tell me about your school"). Interviews used in the traditional quantitative approach are more structured and usually closed-ended ("Which one of the following would you say describes the food in the school cafeteria: 'very good,' 'good,' 'bad,' or 'very bad'?").

In traditional quantitative research, the open-ended interviews are used for early research on issues, when information is not already available. This is especially crucial in research on cross-cultural and multicultural issues, when the psychological repertoire of a population is not readily known. For example, in construction of attitude scales, the open-ended interview is used to obtain statements related to the object of the study. These statements are then organized in the form of an initial "item pool." The items are then used in more structured interviews or questionnaires to measure attitudes and/or opinions (Likert scale, Thurstone scale, and so on).

In traditional qualitative research, the unstructured interviews are used extensively either in an individual setting or in a group setting ("focus group interview"; see Stewardt & Shamdasani, 1990). The responses are usually recorded (audio, video, or both), transcribed, and subjected to "content analysis" (we will discuss the steps in Chapter 6).

Despite the dichotomy of classification by some writers, many research interviews combine the open- and closed-ended interview formats. The most common type of combination is a "funnel interview" in which the researcher starts with very broad questions and gradually limits the scope of the questions to a few focused issues. This type of interview is directly applicable to the mixed research approach.

The interview is a powerful method of data collection. It provides one-to-one interaction between you (or your data collectors) and the individuals you are studying (or a small number of participants in a focus group; see Krueger, 1988). It provides an opportunity to ask for clarification if an answer is vague or to provide clarification if a question is not clear. Open-ended interviews result in copious information about issues. Such information might lead to conceptualization of the issues in ways totally different from what you anticipated.

Interviews have major drawbacks and disadvantages too. They are time-consuming and expensive. Only a small number of interviews can be conducted for a dissertation research project without external financial support. This problem may be partially solved by using a combination of computers and telecommunication devices to conduct interviews; see Lavrakas (1993) for details of such applications. One of the major disadvantages of the interview is the risk of interviewer effects on responses of the interviewee. You might unknowingly affect the responses through gestures, mannerism, or verbal feedback. If you (the researcher) are also the interviewer, there is a danger of showing subtle signs of agreement with statements and/or responses that are anticipated. Such effects are less pronounced in telephone interviews; however, the telephone interviewer might still affect the responses verbally. See Lavrakas (1993) for strategies to reduce such effects.

To the issues involved in interviewing, you can also add the "reactivity" problems discussed before. Additionally, the recording of the obtained information might be affected by your expectations, especially if you have to make inferences regarding the interviewees' attributes (e.g., traits, motivations) based on your observations during the interview. Finally, the analysis of open-ended interviews is more costly and time-consuming than for closed-ended interviews or questionnaires. For a discussion of strategies to reduce these problems, see Fowler and Mangione (1990, especially chap. 9).

Despite these drawbacks, the interview is frequently the best method of data collection among individuals who cannot read or write well, such as children. It is also most appropriately used in situations in which an in-depth knowledge of issues and relationships is needed such as in novel circumstances or interviews with unfamiliar cultural groups. Cross-cultural and multicultural research is a prime example of such applications.

Questionnaires. Questionnaires are mainly paper-and-pencil methods of data collection. With the advent of personal computers (PCs), they are now also widely used for presenting the questions and recording the responses. Depending on the complexity of issues being researched, both the paper-and-pencil and the computerized forms of questionnaires may require a level of sophistication and reading ability that might not be present in the individuals who are being studied. In large-scale survey studies, questionnaires are sometimes "read" to a small number of respondents who cannot read or write well.

An advantage of questionnaires is that you can mail them to your research participants. Mail surveys are less expensive to conduct than interviews or personally administered questionnaires. However, you must typically use an extensive method of follow-up consisting of two to three reminders along with at least one or two consequent mailings of the questionnaire to the nonrespondents (see Ary et al., 1996; Mangione, 1995, for a list of steps for mail surveys). Despite most efforts, some people will never respond. This "attrition" from your original sample might be a threat to the generalizability (external validity) and inference quality (internal validity) of your conclusions, especially if the nonrespondents are systematically different from the rest of the population (e.g., certain ethnicities, certain types of beliefs). For a discussion of problems pertaining to attrition and nonresponse in this respect, and possible ways of reducing and eliminating them, see Mangione (1995, chap. 7).

Similar to interviews, questionnaires may also have different forms and cover a variety of issues. For instance, questionnaires might combine closed- and open-ended items. Open-ended items have different levels of "openness." Some items might ask for a one-word response to a specific question while other items might ask for many sentences (see Fowler, 1993, chap. 5, for a discussion of ways to construct good items). Also, questionnaires might ask questions in different formats. A frequently used format is similar to multiple-choice items ("Please select one of the following that best represents your educational plans for the future"). Items might also be in the form of checklists, with respondents asked to check all options that apply to them.

Personality questionnaires, inventories, and checklists. Most personality inventories might also be considered forms of questionnaires. They are used for measurement of personality attributes of the respondents. These attributes are theoretically expected to be somewhat stable and differentiate individuals from each other. Most personality attributes are considered to be "traits" rather than "states." A "state" attribute is expected to be more short term and dependent on a specific situation than a "trait." A detailed description of personality inventories is beyond the scope of this book (see Barnett & Macmann, 1990, for a review). The Keirsey Temperament Sorter (Keirsey & Bates, 1984) is an example of a personality trait inventory. Other, more informal and more commonly used measures are measures of self-perceptions, locus of control (internal versus external), and self-efficacy (see Robinson, Shaver, & Wrightsman, 1991, for some examples).

An increasing number of researchers in education, psychology, and other behavioral sciences use these scales to collect data regarding personal attributes that might be related to behaviors. An example of this is the measurement of "teachers' sense of efficacy" and its relationship to participation in decision making (Taylor & Tashakkori, 1995, 1997) or acceptance of behavioral intervention (Hughes, Barker, Kemenoff, & Hart, 1996). Another example is the relationship between self-efficacy and a variety of health-related behaviors such as using birth control, protected sex, and similar actions (see Brien, Dennis, Mahoney, & Wallnau, 1994; Joffe & Radius, 1993).

Attitude scales. Attitude scales are questionnaires commonly used in survey research. Although construction of a formal attitude scale is difficult and time-consuming, scales used in previous research are abundant (see Robinson & Shaver, 1975; Robinson et al., 1991, for examples). These scales include measures of attitudes, beliefs, self-perceptions, intentions, aspirations, and a variety of related constructs. Researchers who use *one* type of such scales in their research typically employ a *Likert-type* or an *Osgood-type* (semantic differential) scale. You will find a summary of the procedures for construction of these two (and other types) of scales in Ary et al. (1996) or Gall et al. (1996).

Likert-type scales ask the respondents to express their degree of agreement/ disagreement with issues (or presence/absence of an attribute) on response scales consisting of 4 or 5 options ("strongly agree," "agree," "disagree," or "strongly disagree"). A number is assigned to each response (e.g., +2, +1, −1, −2, according to the direction and magnitude of agreement). You then add up all item scores to obtain an overall attitude score for the questionnaire or for each section of it.

In *Osgood-type* (semantic differential) scales, the respondents are asked to express their reactions to an attitude object (e.g., "site-based management" or "social studies") by putting a mark on each of a set of bipolar adjective scales (e.g., "Useful _ _ _ _ Useless"). You assign numbers to each of these responses (e.g., +2, +1, −1, −2) and add these numbers up to obtain an overall attitude score. An advantage of Osgood-type scales is that the same set of bipolar adjectives can be used to measure attitudes regarding a variety of attitude objects (e.g., replace "social studies" with "math" at the top of the page and use the same adjectives).

Indirect self-reports: Projective techniques. These measurement instruments are all based on the assumption that, when faced with an ambiguous situation, people's reactions reflect their feelings, beliefs, and tendencies, which are not expressed in response to direct questions. A detailed description of these methods is beyond the scope of this book. Traditional examples in psychology are the use of *inkblots* (for example, the Holtzman Inkblot Technique; see Chandler, 1990, for a review). Projective interpretation of children's drawing is another example in child psychology and related disciplines (see Knoff, 1990, for some examples). Another frequently used method is sentence completion, in which individuals are presented with incomplete sentences about specific issues and are asked to complete them (see Haak, 1990, for some examples). These responses are then subjected to "content analysis" (see Chapter 6).

Seeing What People Do: Observational Methods

Despite their advantages, self-report measures have a major disadvantage of being affected by the person who is reporting (i.e., participant reactivity, discussed above). Often, observational methods attempt to reduce these effects by directly observing behaviors rather than asking the individual about them. Obviously, there are many attributes, motivations, feelings, and so on that cannot be inferred from behaviors. Hence observations are more useful if they are combined with other methods of collecting information.

Participant observation. "Participant," "naturalistic," and "ethnographic" observation have been used to identify a variety of data collection methods in which researchers observe behaviors or events in their natural setting and record them (e.g., Rosnow & Rosenthal, 1996; Spradley, 1979). In all of these observational methods, the researcher is an active participant in the interpersonal environment of the unit that is being observed. The main objective of the researcher is to measure/document the behaviors and interaction patterns as they occur in the "natural setting."

Nonparticipant observation. These are observations in which the researcher is not an "active" part of the setting in which the behaviors and/or interactions are being observed. An example is observation of children's play behavior through one-way mirrors. Another example, deemed unethical in research, is recording through concealed cameras and/or tape recorders. Although a new phenomenon, "observation" of Internet users for marketing and/or other purposes by recording the pattern and frequency of their access to different sites is another example. Ethical considerations regarding use of these data for research purposes require serious consideration.

An interesting, and very recent, trend in indirect observation is the use of small computers to monitor behaviors, heart rate, and/or hormonal changes. For example, a number of small new gadgets are being field-tested in different countries to monitor the pattern/frequency of women taking birth control pills. The data are recorded and later downloaded by the researcher for analysis. These indirect and nonparticipant methods of "observation" are becoming increasingly sophisticated.

A specific type of nonparticipant observation consists of observing the outcome of behaviors and making inferences regarding actors, their preferences, and/or behaviors. These "unobtrusive measures" are usually obtained long after the individuals have left the setting of the behavior (some writers—for example, Babbie, 1996—have classified archival data and documents as forms of unobtrusive observations, while we prefer to discuss them in a separate section below). As an example, one might investigate the type of books that the students in a high school check out of the library. Another classic example is the observation of the degree of wear and tear on the carpet in a museum to find out which sections are more popular (e.g., Patton, 1990). Such indirect observations are useful for measuring those variables that might be affected by normative pressures and/or social desirability. Generally speaking, these unobtrusive observations do not involve the tough ethical dilemmas facing the more general nonparticipant observations.

Advantages and disadvantages of the observational method. Observations eliminate the need to ask individuals about their behaviors or tendencies, and reduce the possibility of controlled responses. However, reactivity problems are not eliminated. In addition to the different reactivity effects discussed above, awareness of being observed might have other social-psychological effects on individuals. A classic example is what Duval and Wicklund (1972) have called "objective self-awareness." According to their framework, when a person is being observed, he or she becomes more aware of the inconsistency between his or her behaviors and his or her values (or perceived norms). This, in turn, leads to different types of inferences regarding the causality of his or her behaviors, and might also lead to unintentional changes in behaviors or reactions to the social environment.

It is difficult (and often risky) to make inferences regarding a person's intentions, motivations, and/or other unobservable attributes on the basis of observable reactions and behaviors. Much of our social perceptions are concentrated around understanding the causality of behaviors of other people. As researchers, we are not immune to erroneous tendencies that are inherent in such perceptions. A well-known example of such tendencies is the "actor-observer difference" in attributions (Jones & Nisbett, 1972). According to social-psychological research, there might be major contradictions between an observer's inferences regarding the reasons an actor behaved in a certain way as compared with that actor's own perceptions regarding these causes. As actors, we generally attribute the causality of our behaviors to factors in the context ("external causes"), while observers would attribute these same behaviors to factors unique to us (our dispositions, beliefs, or "internal causes"). The implication of these perceptual tendencies is that, as observers, we might consider other people's behaviors more as a result of their attitudes, personality, intentions, and so on than as their reactions to the situation.

In both QUAL and QUAN research, observations are often used as means of obtaining information regarding the observed participant's behaviors rather than viewpoints and/or perceptions regarding causality of behaviors. The perceptual tendencies mentioned above may not be applicable to such observations. Furthermore, for QUAL researchers, the point of view of the *observed* participant, rather than of the observer/researcher, is of primary interest. Hence such perceptions are identified and recorded through interviews or other self-report sources of *firsthand* information (e.g., diaries, writings). In Chapter 4, we presented different strategies for ensuring the quality of data and inferences in QUAL research. Such strategies (e.g., *member checks*) will further guard you against possible effects of the perceptual errors mentioned above.

*Asking Individuals About Their
Relationship With Others: Sociometry*

You can use sociometry to get a "snapshot" of interpersonal interaction and/or communication in a group. Each member of a group or organization is asked to specify with whom he or she interacts or is willing to interact/ cooperate under different circumstances. A *sociogram* is then developed to represent the complex net of interactions or interrelationships between group members. A sociogram is a graphic representation of these interactions or communications. A more detailed application of sociometry is presented in Chapter 8 when we discuss Durland's (1996) dissertation.

Sociometry does not have some of the reactivity problems of self-report measures. One reason is that the group members are not asked about the structure of the group (e.g., who is popular, who is not liked). Each group member is asked to identify one or two other group members with whom he or she interacts or will interact if he or she has a chance. Also, it is usually difficult for a single member of the group to construe (i.e., make sense of) the complex structure of interpersonal dynamics in the group.

A sociogram has limitations too. It usually does not provide information regarding the *reasons* that specific patterns of interaction exist in the group. Many of these reasons are identified through follow-up interviews and/or field observations. Furthermore, as the size of the group increases, the complexity of a sociogram increases exponentially. Hence it becomes extremely difficult to make inferences regarding larger organizations and groups. Complex methods of computerized analysis, graphing, and calculating statistical indicators have been developed and are available to researchers. For details of these, see Wasserman and Faust (1994) and Durland (1996).

*Using Data Collected and/or Documented by Others:
Archival Data and Meta-Analysis*

Archival data are the data collected and/or documented by individuals and/or institutions regarding individuals and/or groups. Examples of such data are the school records regarding students, clinic records regarding patients, city records of marriages and divorces, a library's collection of "oral histories" regarding a specific entity, or a person's autobiography. Obviously, these might be in the form of numerical data and/or narrative information about the units of investigation.[2]

Before you analyze any archival data to answer research questions, you must ask the two major questions regarding the quality of such information (i.e., validity and reliability). Two additional questions should be asked regarding most historical and archival information as well as oral histories: "Were the data recorded accurately?" and "Were the data kept in their entirety?" If information is not recorded accurately or is only recorded selectively for some individuals/cases, the internal validity or trustworthiness of your conclusions will be suspect. The same is true if some information is kept but some is not. For example, if school records do not contain the files of those who dropped out or were expelled, the internal validity (trustworthiness) of the conclusions will be questionable.

The information gathered for "meta-analysis" consists of what other studies have found regarding an issue or question. Quantitative meta-analysis is a synthesis of a relatively large number of studies to get an estimate of the strength of relationship between variables *(effect size)* across these studies, and the degree to which effects/relationships vary across these empirical studies. In the majority of applications, meta-analysis is not considered to be a data collection strategy. It is, instead, considered a method of data analysis. For details, see Rosenthal (1991).

Although meta-analysis is often considered a QUAN research method, the general method (i.e., using previous studies as units of analysis) is applicable to QUAL research as well. For example, instead of determining the *effect size,* the investigator might determine a typology or classification of *themes* in the findings of a set of studies.

Multiple modes of data collection. There is no doubt about the benefits of multiple methods of data collection and multiple sources of data. As much as the "realities of the field" permit, most studies, regardless of QUAL/QUAN designation, take advantage of these multiple methods. For example, in both single-subject experimental studies (quantitative) and qualitative case studies (see Yin, 1994), it is possible to collect data from a variety of sources (participants, parents, teachers, and so on) and through a variety of methods such as observation, interview, and standard tests (for more information regarding "single-case research," see Franklin, Allison, & Gorman, 1996). Similarly, experimental and ethnographic researchers have the opportunity to obtain multiple types of data (observation, interview, archival, and so on) from multiple sources (in lab experiments, these other sources might be other participants in the study). Even in the large-scale survey studies such as the National Education Longitudinal Study of 1988 (NELS-88; Ingles et al., 1992), data are gathered from multiple sources (students, parents, teachers, school) and a variety of measurement formats (attitudinal survey, achievement tests, school transcripts, other archival data).

Your research method (e.g., experimental, survey, ethnography) might impose *some* limitation on the type of data collection procedure you can use. However, you can find creative ways of collecting data through multiple methods and multiple sources. Such creativity is possible only if you are well familiar with different research procedures/designs. Most textbooks on research methods will provide you with details of these.

A source of data, which is usually ignored, is your personal knowledge about a culture, a group, or an organization. Although this knowledge is not systematically measured, it provides an auxiliary source of data that can enrich your collected data. In our own research, we have frequently used anecdotal cultural observations and experiences as "informal" sources of such data. In cross-cultural and multicultural research, these "cultural observations" usually guide the interpretation of results that are obtained through surveys or other methods. Although these "expert" observations are not classified as "data," they are forms of QUAL (inferential) data. As such, we believe that cross-cultural and multicultural studies, even the highly quantitative ones, are inherently mixed.

An example comes from some of our own ongoing research (Tashakkori, Aghajanian, & Mehryar, 1996; Tashakkori & Thompson, 1991; Tashakkori, Thompson, & Mehryar, 1987). During more than 20 years (1974, 1982, 1984, 1986, and 1996), we have collected five survey data sets among adolescents in southern Iran. In each of these surveys, we have measured attitudes and intentions/plans regarding education, marriage, childbearing, and labor market participation of women. We have compared these results across the five time periods with gender and SES backgrounds. Our knowledge of the sociocultural changes across the past three decades and our cultural observations during that period have been significant tools for the interpretation of the survey data.

Results suggest a steady trend toward modernization in the 1970s, followed by a sharp reduction of such trends in the early 1980s. However, contrary to the predictions of some of our colleagues, the results also point to a relatively strong return of attitudinal and behavioral modernity in the 1990s, especially among women. Without detailed cultural observations and knowledge, interpretation of these seemingly inconsistent trends and changes would be impossible or, at best, inaccurate. For a mixed model researcher, even when inferences are based on highly systematic quantitative data, personal observations of the context of data collection as well as interactions with the individuals who are the sources of data are valuable sources of information. Even in highly structured experimental studies, such observations provide additional strength to the quality of inferences on the basis of the results.

NOTES

1. It should be noted that in some QUAL research, the participants play a much more active role in the process, becoming coresearchers of the researcher.

2. A large amount of information is available in public domain data sets. These data are collected at the national, state, or even international levels. These may also be considered archival data for researchers who do "secondary analysis." Examples of these data sets in the United States are the *General Social Survey* (GSS) and the National Education Longitudinal Study of Eighth Grade (NLS-88). International examples include a variety of data that are collected in different countries every year by the United Nations, the World Bank, and private organizations as well as the census data and similar data sets that are made available by the governments. For a comprehensive discussion of the methods of analysis for such data, see Stewart and Kamins (1993).

6

Alternatives to Traditional Data Analytic Strategies

In this chapter, we first present an overview of data analysis strategies in quantitative and qualitative research traditions. Strengths and weaknesses of each general approach will be discussed. Then we discuss alternative ways of combining the two types of analysis in one study, along with examples from the literature.

As discussed in Chapter 4, data analysis and presentation strategies are dependent on the scale of measurement for the variables under study. For nominal and qualitative-narrative variables, qualitative data analysis techniques are appropriate. Nonparametric statistics are methods of data analysis for most ordinal-level variables, while parametric methods are mainly used for interval-level variables. Despite these distinctions, parametric numerical analyses are also frequently used for variables that are *theoretically* interval variables, even though their obtained measurement results might be ordinal.

TRADITIONAL QUANTITATIVE DATA ANALYSIS

Most traditional methods of data analysis can be summarized in the form of a 2 × 2 Quantitative Data Analysis Matrix that crosses two dimensions: (a) whether the statistic is used for determining the relationship between variables or differences between groups and (b) whether the statistic is appropriate for use with interval or noninterval data. This simplified presentation should prove beneficial for novice researchers, while more sophisticated researchers probably have their own method of categorizing statistical procedures. We present this table here to introduce different "families" of statistical procedures that will be elaborated upon later in this chapter.

While this 2×2 matrix is useful as an overview of the various "families" of statistical procedures, the remainder of this discussion of quantitative analytical techniques will focus on two other dichotomies:

1. descriptive versus inferential methods
2. univariate versus multivariate methods

Descriptive Methods

These methods include presentations of results through simple statistics and graphic displays. The main objective of these analyses is to provide images and/or summaries that can help the reader understand the nature of the variables and their relationships. The most commonly used methods of descriptive data analysis and presentation are (a) measures of central tendency, (b) measures of relative standing, and (c) measures of association/relationship between variables.

Measures of central tendency summarize a group of observations/scores into a single score. Mode, mean, and median are all measures of central tendency and are single scores that represent groups of events/people. *Mode* is the most frequent score in a group. *Mean* is the average of scores (sum divided by number of scores). *Median* is the score at or below which 50% of the scores fall (it divides the group of scores into two equal halves).

What measure of central tendency is better? The answer depends on the type of measurement scale. Mode is a simple measure that is understandable to everybody; however, it only represents one score. It does not provide information regarding the rest of the scores.

Because the mean is the average of *all* scores in the distribution, it contains information regarding all members of the group. Despite this advantage, the mean has two disadvantages. First, it can only be calculated for variables that are measured on an ordinal or higher scale. For example, the "mean" gender of a group of males and females is not meaningful. Second, extreme scores skew the mean.

The median is the score in the middle of the distribution. For example, if the ages of a group of adults who are attending an Alcoholics Anonymous (A.A.) meeting are 17, 19, 20, 56, and 59, the median age of this group would be 20. This figure (20) is very different from the mean age of the group (34.2) and obviously presents a different image of the group. Adding two new members to the group, one with the age of 16 and the other with the age of 85, will not change the median score. This is because the median does not include information regarding the other scores in the distribution.

This is a disadvantage in some cases but an advantage when there ar extreme scores in the distribution, such as the 85-year-old A.A. memb

Measures of variability include average deviation, variance, stand deviation, and the interquartile range. Average deviation, variance, standard deviation are all based on the number of units of differe between each score and the mean. They represent the degree to which scores are "bunched around" the mean of the distribution (see Gravette Wallnau, 1998, for a review). They are based on deviation scores (e score's distance from the mean). Average deviation is the simple aver of these deviations when the +/– sign of the deviations are ignored (: average deviation is the mean of the absolute values of deviations).

If you square each deviation, add all of these squared deviations, a divide the sum of squared deviations by the number of scores, you w obtain variance (i.e., variance is the mean of the squared deviations). T square root of the variance is conceptually similar to the average deviatic and is called the standard deviation. It is used more frequently than th average deviation because it is more amenable to mathematical manipula tion than the average deviation.

Measures of relative standing are single indicators of the relative pos tion of a score in relation to others. Percentile rank is one of them Percentile rank simply shows what percentage of scores fall at or below specific score. For example, if a child's mathematics score on the Californi Achievement Test has a percentile rank of 68, it means that child's score i better than 68% of children in the group that was tested. Percentile rank i easy to understand but has a major drawback: Differences between ranks do not represent differences in ability (or the underlying attribute). For example, a difference of 2 percentile ranks (e.g., $70 - 68 = 2$) does not have the same meaning as the same difference of 2 between other ranks (for example $88 - 86 = 2$).

Standard scores are free from this drawback. An example is the z-score. A difference of 2 z-scores ($3 - 1 = 2$) has the same meaning regardless of the magnitude of the original scores (for example, it represents the same gap in the magnitude of the attribute as the difference of 2 points between two other z-scores, such as $2.8 - 0.8 = 2$). A person's z-score is based on the deviation of his or her score from the mean of the distribution. You obtain a z-score by dividing that deviation by the standard deviation of the distribution (i.e., you convert the person's deviation score into units of standard deviation).

Measures of association/relationship are single indicators of the degree of relationship between two or more variables. The Pearson correlation (r) is the most widely used example. The Pearson correlation ranges from

Table 6.1

The Quantitative Data Analysis Matrix:
A Simplified Typology of Quantitative Data Analysis Techniques
Used in Behavioral and Social Sciences

of Data	Relationship Between Variables	Differences Between Groups
al/Ordinal	Pearson correlation (r)	t-test for independent samples
	Multiple correlation	ANOVA/ANCOVA
	Canonical correlation	MANOVA/MANCOVA
	Regression analysis	Discriminant analysis
	Factor analysis	
nal/Nominal	Rho	Sign test
	Chi-square test of independence/association	Wilcoxon matched pairs
	Phi	
	Cramer's V	
	Logistic regression	

(perfect negative relationship) to +1 (perfect positive relationship). A
rrelation close to zero means there is no relationship. As indicated in
ıble 6.1, there are a variety of other statistics in the family of correlations
.g., rho, phi; see Gravetter & Wallnau, 1998).

ıferential Methods

Descriptive statistics, graphs, or combinations of the two are not suffi-
ient for most research purposes. Specifically, these methods are not
ufficient for estimation and testing hypotheses. Data analysis methods for
ɔsting hypotheses are based on estimations of how much *error* is involved
n obtaining a difference between groups, or a relationship between vari-
ıbles. These data analysis methods are usually classified as *inferential
statistics*. An example of these methods is the *t*-test for testing the significance of differences between two group means, discussed in more detail
below.

In inferential statistical analysis, tests of statistical significance provide
information regarding the possibility that the results happened "just by
chance and random error" versus their occurrence due to some fundamental
true relationship between variables. If the results (e.g., differences between
means) are statistically significant, then the researcher concludes that they
did not occur solely by chance. The basic assumption in such hypothesis
testing is that any apparent relationship between variables (or difference

between groups) might, in fact, be due to random fluctuations in measurement of the variables or in individuals who are observed/studied. Inferential statistics are methods of estimating the degree of such chance variation. In addition, these methods of data analysis provide information regarding the magnitude of the effect, or the relationship. A brief summary of these methods follows:

1. Testing differences between group means:
    a. comparing the mean of a sample with the mean of a population: z-test
    b. comparing the means of two samples:
        (1) independent sets of observations: t-test for independent groups
        (2) nonindependent sets of observations (matched groups, repeated observations, and so on): t-test for nonindependent groups
    c. comparing the means of two or more samples or comparing means in factorial designs (those with more than one independent variable): analysis of variance (ANOVA)
    d. comparing the means of two or more samples while controlling for the variation due to an extraneous variable: analysis of covariance (ANCOVA)
2. Determining if correlation coefficients (or regression slopes) are truly different from zero:
    a. t-test for the significance of Pearson r from zero
    b. F-test for the significance of multiple correlation
    c. t- or F-test for the significance of slopes in multiple regression analysis

Univariate Versus Multivariate Methods

Examples and discussions in the previous section concerned univariate statistics. These statistics are based on one (dependent) variable or, in the case of *bivariate* correlations, they represent the relationship between two single variables. Much research in the social and behavioral sciences addresses the relationship among more than two single variables. For example, assume that you are interested in finding the correlation between a variable (such as college GPA) from a *combination* of other variables (such as high school GPA, parental education, and parental income). In the college GPA example, you need to use *multiple correlation (R)*. Multiple correlation is still a univariate statistic, and its interpretation is very similar to the bivariate (Pearson) correlation.

In multiple correlation (or multiple regression), there is a set of variables on one side of the equation and a single variable on the other side. Sometimes researchers are interested in associating multiple variables on *both* sides of the equation. When the correlation between two sets (combinations) of variables is being investigated, a *canonical correlation* would be the statistic of choice. For example, you might be interested in determining the canonical correlation between self-efficacy, academic self-concept, and last year's GPA with the combination of three indicators of achievement (math, science, and reading) among high school students. Canonical correlation is a multivariate statistic.

Examples of other multivariate methods are *discriminant function analysis* and *factor analysis.* In discriminant function analysis, the objective is to find an optimal set of variables that differentiate two or more groups from each other. For example, what variables differentiate the eighth grade students who drop out of school and those who continue to the tenth grade?

In exploratory factor analysis, the objective is to determine the underlying dimensions (constructs) of a set of measures/variables. In confirmatory factor analysis (and numerous variations or extensions of it, such as in structural equations modeling), the objective is to ascertain if the predicted structure of the construct is obtained in the data. (See Stevens, 1996, and Harris, 1985, for more information regarding multivariate methods.)

TRADITIONAL QUALITATIVE DATA ANALYSIS

As with quantitative data, there are a variety of established procedures for analyzing qualitative data. These narrative data are usually prepared for analysis by converting raw material (e.g., field notes, documents, audio-tapes) into partially processed data (e.g., write-ups, transcripts), which are then coded and subjected to a particular analysis scheme (Huberman & Miles, 1994).

These analysis schemes may be differentiated on two dimensions: (a) whether the themes or categories were established a priori or emerged during the analysis and (b) the degree of complexity of the qualitative analysis scheme (ranging from simple to complex). Table 6.2 contains a presentation of the Qualitative Data Analysis Matrix that is generated by crossing these two dimensions, plus a few illustrative cases of specific strategies for analyzing qualitative data.

Before describing some of these specific strategies for analyzing qualitative data, a few comments will be made concerning the two dimensions that constitute the Qualitative Data Analysis Matrix. This matrix contains examples of schemes that have been used by a variety of analysts to make sense of narrative data. These analysts approach qualitative data from a

Table 6.2

The Qualitative Data Analysis Matrix: A Simplified Typology of
Qualitative Data Analysis Techniques in the Behavioral and Social Sciences

Type of Theme	More Simple Schemes	More Complex Schemes
A priori	Simple valence analysis, manifest content analysis	Effects matrices (Miles & Huberman, 1994)
Emerging	Latent content analysis, constant comparative analysis (Glaser & Strauss, 1967; Lincoln & Guba, 1985)	Developmental research sequence (Spradley, 1979, 1980)

variety of different orientations, including the postpositivistic and prag-
matic as well as the constructivistic.

For example, Huberman and Miles (1994), in a chapter on data management and analysis in the *Handbook of Qualitative Research,* referred to
themselves as "transcendental realists" who "believe that social phenomena exist not only in the mind, but in the objective world as well, and that
there are some lawful, reasonably stable relationships to be found among
them" (p. 429). Huberman and Miles further stated that qualitative data can
be analyzed either inductively or deductively, depending upon the stage of
the research cycle in which the analyst is working. Miles and Huberman's
(1994) own scheme for analyzing qualitative data, gathered in assessing
educational innovations, involves setting up what they call "effects matrices" in advance, based on their previous experiences in analyzing data of
this type.

This point of view is antithetical to the canons of the constructivists, who
believe that inductive logic should be used exclusively in analyzing qualitative data and that themes should emerge from the data and not be
determined a priori (e.g., Lincoln & Guba, 1985). For example, Lincoln
and Guba (1985) presented an expanded version of the constant comparative method, which was first discussed by Glaser and Strauss (1967), as
their method for analyzing qualitative data. This system uses inductive
logic to develop emerging themes or categories from a mass of narrative
data. These authors probably would not consider the a priori matrices of
Miles and Huberman (1994) appropriate for analyzing qualitative data
because they are based on deductively derived categories.

With regard to the complexity dimension, there is a continuum among
the various schemes in the Qualitative Data Analysis Matrix. An example
of the most basic schemes is simple valence analysis (Teddlie, Kirby, &

Stringfield, 1989) in which there were three predetermined categories for coding qualitative data gathered during classroom observations. A much more complex analysis scheme is the Developmental Research Sequence described by Spradley (1979, 1980). This emerging themes scheme involves 12 steps, including three distinct levels of progressively more involved analyses (domain, taxonomic, componential).

The Emphasis on Developing Categories or Themes

The essence of qualitative data analysis of any type is the development of a typology of categories or themes that summarize a mass of narrative data. As Huberman and Miles (1994) stated,

> Qualitative studies ultimately aim to describe and explain (at some level) a pattern of relationships, which can be done only with a set of conceptually specified analytical categories (Mishler, 1990). Starting with them (deductively) or getting gradually to them (inductively) are both legitimate and useful paths. (p. 431)

Of interest, there appears to be some regularity in the numbers of categories that arise in many cases in which an emerging themes analysis is undertaken. Typically, when analyzing data sets with 200 or fewer units of information with regard to one particular open-ended question, around six to eight categories emerge. The initial number of categories emerging from such a database may be 10 to 15, but through combining similar groups of responses and developing more inclusive definitions, the number can be reduced to 6 to 8. This analytical phenomenon may be due partially to the limit in the capacity that we as a species have for understanding the complexities of any topic.

Examples of A Priori Themes Analyses

In Table 6.2, there were three examples of a priori themes analyses: simple valence analysis, manifest content analysis, and the effects matrices of Miles and Huberman (1994).

Simple Valence Analysis

Simple valence analysis is the least complex of all the categorical schemes presented in Table 6.2. It was used by Teddlie et al. (1989) in an analysis of a rather large database consisting of classroom observations gathered during a longitudinal study of school effectiveness. More than 700 classroom observations were conducted using an open-ended instrument with 15 items representing general indicators of teaching effectiveness. Therefore, there were more than 10,000 open-ended responses to analyze from this database. To expedite the analysis, the researchers used a coding scheme in which two raters analyzed a sample of the responses and coded each response into three predetermined categories:

1. The response contained evidence of effective teaching behavior regarding this particular teaching component.
2. The response contained evidence of contradictory teaching behavior regarding this particular teaching component.
3. The response indicated an absence of effective teaching behavior regarding this particular teaching component.

Patton (1990) called this type of coding scheme an "analyst-constructed typology." Later in this chapter, the data from this study will be considered again when the mixed analytical technique known as "quantitizing" (Miles & Huberman, 1994) is discussed.

Manifest Content Analysis

There are two types of content analysis: manifest and latent. *Manifest content analysis* was defined by Berelson (1952) as "a research technique for the objective, systematic, and quantitative description of the manifest content of communication" (p. 18). Within the positivistically oriented fields of sociology and mass communication during the 1950s and 1960s, this type of content analysis was narrowly defined as a "quantitatively oriented technique whereby standardized measurements are applied to metrically defined units and these are used to characterize and compare documents" (Manning & Cullum-Swan, 1994, p. 464). Examples include the analysis and comparison of textbooks, popular magazines and newspapers, writings of the classic authors (e.g., Shakespeare), and political speeches.

The coding procedures for these comparative analyses are standardized to the highest degree possible. Gall et al. (1996) described the procedure as follows:

Once the content has been selected using appropriate sampling techniques, a coding or classification system needs to be developed for analyzing the content. When possible, use a coding system that has already been developed in previous research. First, this option saves the time needed to develop your own system, which for most content-analysis studies is a difficult and time-consuming task. Also, the use of standard coding categories permits comparisons with other studies that have used the same system. (pp. 525-526)

An example of content analysis dictionaries is the *Harvard III Psychosocial Dictionary,* which is used in psychology and sociology. It contains content categories in areas such as cultural processes, social-emotional actions, roles, and psychological processes.

For many research projects, such highly structured content analysis dictionaries are not available. Indeed, content analysis is more typically discussed in the 1990s as a generic way of analyzing any type of narrative data; for example, Patton (1990) referred to content analysis as the analysis of qualitative data in general and contrasted it with the statistical analysis of quantitative data. Researchers in the social and behavioral sciences typically have to develop their own coding schemes a priori or allow them to emerge within their own research studies.

The distinction between the manifest and latent content of a document refers to the difference between the surface meaning of a text and the underlying meaning of that narrative. For example, one could count the number of violent acts (defined a priori) that occur during a television program and make conclusions concerning the degree of manifest violence that was demonstrated in the program. To truly understand the underlying latent content of the violence within a specific program, however, the "context" (Manning & Cullum-Swan, 1994) within which the program occurred would have to be analyzed. In this case, that context would be the narrative or plot of the program. A television program with several violent scenes, yet with an underlying theme of trust or concern among the characters, might generate a latent content analysis very different from its manifest content analysis.

Within the Qualitative Data Analysis Matrix presented in Table 6.2, manifest content analysis was categorized as an a priori themes process, while latent content analysis was categorized as an emerging themes process. For example, the categories for the manifest content of high school history textbooks could be predetermined and might involve topics such as the democratic ideal, westward expansion, slavery, or manifest destiny. The latent content for these high school history textbooks, on the other hand, would not be determinable in advance of actually analyzing the data. More examples of latent content analysis will be given in the next section.

The Effects Matrices of Miles and Huberman

The Miles and Huberman (1994) volume titled *Qualitative Data Analysis* emphasized placing qualitative data into matrices that were either developed before data collection or in the early stages of data collection. These a priori codes and matrices were developed from several years of work that these authors had done within the field of educational innovation. Their a priori coding scheme included categories such as the properties of innovations, the external context of the innovation, the internal context of the innovation, the adoption process, and site dynamics and transformations. They developed a rather extensive list of codes to categorize each piece of narrative data that they collected. For example, one such code was "Internal Context: Norms and Authority," which had the acronym IC:NORM; each unit of information that fell into that category was therefore coded IC:NORM.

Their matrices involved crossing the levels of one of their coding categories by the levels of another category. For example, one matrix might cross assistance location by type of assistance.

Miles and Huberman (1994) presented qualitative data analysis as having three parts: (a) *data reduction,* or taking the raw data and simplifying and transforming them using the aforementioned *codes*; (b) *data display,* which is displaying the data in an organized assembly of information that permits the drawing of conclusions (the *effects matrices* are used in this stage of analysis); and (c) *conclusion drawing and verification,* or deciding what everything means and determining the validity of those conclusions.

Examples of Emerging Themes Analyses

In Table 6.2, there were three examples of emerging themes analyses: latent content analysis, constant comparative analysis, and the Developmental Research Sequence.

Latent Content Analysis

As noted above, *manifest content* refers to the surface meaning of a text while *latent content* refers to the underlying meaning of that narrative. The latent content of a text is determined by a subjective evaluation of the overall content of the narrative. In the example above, the manifest content of the violence of a television program could be easily determined by simply counting the number of violent acts that occurred during that program. The definition of a violent act would be very precisely determined before the data collection occurred, and this definition would be used to judge many different programs.

The latent content of a television program would be much more difficult to determine, and in most cases that determination could not be made based on a simple a priori coding scheme. The plot of the program would have to be scrutinized and then an analysis scheme appropriate to that particular program would, one hopes, emerge. For instance, a program that dealt with the kidnaping of a young woman by a gang might receive a very high violence rating based on a manifest content analysis because the threat of violence was apparent throughout the program. On the other hand, suppose that the young woman developed a positive, empathic relationship with one of her captors, who freed her at the end of the program. The latent content of the program would be far less violent than the manifest content indicated. The scheme for analyzing the themes associated with the entire program would emerge during the analysis of the program itself; they could not be determined a priori, although once established they perhaps then could be used for analyzing the latent content of other programs.

Constant Comparative Analysis

The constant comparative analytical scheme was first developed by Glaser and Strauss (1967) and then refined by Lincoln and Guba (1985). This analytical scheme involves two general processes: (a) *unitizing,* or breaking the text into units of information that will serve as the basis for defining categories, and (b) *categorizing,* or bringing together into provisional categories those units that relate to the same content, devising rules that describe category properties, and rendering each category set internally consistent and the entire set mutually exclusive. The entire categorizing process involves 10 steps, some of which are iterative (Lincoln & Guba, 1985, pp. 347-351).

The Developmental Research Sequence

The Developmental Research Sequence of James Spradley is one of the most complex schemes for determining the themes associated with what he calls a "cultural scene." The 12-step process for analyzing both interview (Spradley, 1979) and observational data (Spradley, 1980) involves three stages of data gathering and three stages of data analysis:

1. Broad *descriptive questions* are first asked; Spradley calls these grand-tour or mini-tour questions.

2. Data based on responses to these descriptive questions are analyzed using *domain analysis.* Cultural domains are composed of three parts: the cover term (the name of a cultural domain), the included terms (the names for smaller domains within a domain), and semantic relationships (the linking of the included terms to the cover term). An example of a semantic relationship is strict inclusion (i.e., being a kind of). For example, freshmen, sophomores, juniors, and seniors are kinds of undergraduate students.

3. *Structural questions* are then asked. These questions involve asking informants how their cultural knowledge is organized; that is, informants are asked about the basic domains or units of their cultural knowledge. These questions are used to confirm or disconfirm the provisional domains developed from the domain analyses and to elicit more terms for verified domains.

4. Data based on responses to structural questions are analyzed using *taxonomic analysis,* which shows the relationships among all included terms in a domain. Often these taxonomies involve several branches with subsets of included terms bifurcating from them.

5. *Contrast questions* allow the ethnographer to discover the dimensions of meaning that informants employ to distinguish events and objects in their world. These questions use the contrast principle by finding out how included terms within a domain or a taxonomy are different from one another. There are several types of these questions, including contrast verification questions, dyadic contrast questions, and triadic contrast questions.

6. Data based on responses to these contrast questions are analyzed using *componential analysis,* which involves the systematic search for the attributes or components of meaning associated with cultural scenes. Spradley (1979) contends that when analysts discover contrasts among the members of a category, these contrasts may be thought of as the attributes or components of meaning for that category. For instance, in one of Spradley's analyses regarding inmates in a prison, he discovered that "mobility" was one of the attributes that distinguished among different types of inmates in a prison population. *Mobility* refers to the ability of inmates to move freely about the prison itself, in the prison yard, outside the prison, and so on. Therefore, the componential analysis revealed that mobility (or freedom of movement) was one of the major themes associated with prison life.

The Use of Similarities and Contrasts

Spradley (1979, p. 157) explicitly defined two of the major principles used in qualitative data analysis: the similarity principle and the contrast principle. The similarity principle states that the meaning of a symbol can be discovered by finding out how it is similar to other symbols. The contrast principle states that the meaning of a symbol can be discovered by finding out how it is different from other symbols.

The similarity principle is used in all of the analytical systems described above. For example, categories are determined by looking for units of information with similar content (constant comparative analysis) or by looking for terms that have somewhat similar meaning (the Developmental Research Sequence). If determining a typology of categories or themes that summarize a mass of narrative data is the essence of qualitative data analysis, then the similarity principle guides that process by allowing the analyst to search for commonalities in the data.

The contrast principle is explicitly used in the Developmental Research Sequence during the componential analysis stage. It is also a part of constant comparative analysis because it guides the search for mutual exclusivity between the categories that emerge.

ALTERNATIVE ANALYTICAL STRATEGIES
FOR MIXED METHODS STUDIES

The main objective of the alternative analytic strategies is to enable the researcher to use both of the traditional types of analysis simultaneously or in a sequence in the same study.

Many of these techniques have already been used extensively by researchers in social and behavioral sciences. Caracelli and Greene's (1993) summary of these techniques is presented in Box 6.1.

We use a somewhat different logic for the classification of mixed data analysis strategies. A summary of these strategies is presented in Table 6.3. The remainder of this chapter is devoted to discussion and examples of these alternative data analysis techniques.

One of the main data analytic strategies in mixed methods is to convert the data that are collected in one of the traditions into the other tradition such that alternative techniques can be used for analyzing the same data. Two aspects of this type of transformation are (a) converting qualitative

---

BOX 6.1
Caracelli and Greene's Summary of
Mixed Data Analysis Strategies

(1) Data transformation: The conversion or transformation of one data type into another so that both can be analyzed together.

(2) Typology development: The analysis of one data type yields a typology (or set of substantive categories) that is then used as a framework applied in analyzing the contrasting data type.

(3) Extreme-case analysis: "Extreme cases" identified from the analysis of one data type and pursued via (additional data collection and) analysis of data of the other type, with the intent of testing and refining the initial explanation for the extreme cases.

(4) Data consolidation/merging: The joint review of both data types to create new or consolidated variables or data sets, which can be expressed in either quantitative or qualitative form. These consolidated variables or data sets are then typically used in further analysis.

SOURCE: From Caracelli and Greene (1993).

---

information into numerical codes that can be statistically analyzed and (b) converting quantitative data into narratives that can be analyzed qualitatively. We refer to the first type of transformation method as *quantitizing techniques* and to the transformed data as *quantitized data.* The second method is referred to as *qualitizing techniques* and the transformed data are *qualitized data.*

Parallel analysis of the *two types* of data (QUAL and QUAN) provides a richer understanding of the variables and their relationships. However, it limits the investigator to *one* type of data analysis (QUAN *or* QUAL) on *each* subset of the data. In many research studies, it might be possible to gain more insight from the data by

1. doing *both* types of data analysis (QUAL *and* QUAN) on the *same* data simultaneously,

2. confirming/expanding the inferences derived from one method of data analysis (e.g., QUAL) through a secondary analysis of the *same* data with a different approach (e.g., QUAN),

3. sequentially using the results obtained through one approach (e.g., classification of individuals into groups through QUAL analysis) as a starting point for the analysis of *other* data with the alternative approach (e.g.,

Table 6.3

Classification of Alternative Mixed Method Data Analysis Strategies

---

(1) *Concurrent mixed analysis:* Simultaneous analysis of QUAL and QUAN data
    (a) Concurrent analysis of different data: *Parallel mixed analysis* (also known as triangulation of data sources)
    (b) Concurrent analysis of the same data: *Quantitizing*
    (c) Concurrent analysis of the same data: *Qualitizing*
(2) *Sequential QUAL-QUAN analysis:* Qualitative data analysis followed by confirmatory quantitative data collection and analysis
    (a) Forming groups of people/settings on the basis of qualitative data/observations, comparing the groups on QUAN data (e.g., MANOVA, cluster analysis, discriminant function analysis)
    (b) Forming groups of attributes/themes through QUAL (e.g., content) analysis, followed by confirmatory QUAN analysis (e.g., factor analysis, structural equations modeling)
    (c) Establishing a theoretical order of relationship/causality through exploratory QUAL analysis, confirming the obtained sequence through QUAN data and analysis (e.g., path analysis, structural equations modeling)*
(3) *Sequential QUAN-QUAL analysis:* Quantitative data analysis followed by qualitative data collection and analysis
    (a) Forming groups of people/settings on the basis of QUAN data (e.g., cluster analysis), comparing the groups on QUAL data*
    (b) Forming groups of attributes/themes through exploratory QUAN analysis (e.g., factor analysis, multidimensional scaling), confirming with available/new QUAL data and analysis (e.g., constant comparative method)
    (c) Establishing a theoretical order of relationship/causality through exploratory QUAN analysis (path analysis, structural equation modeling, and so on), confirming the obtained sequence through QUAL data and analysis (e.g., observations and interviews with individuals)*

---

*These two strategies need further development in the future. They are presented here tentatively and are not discussed in the text.

statistically compare the groups that were identified by QUAL observations), or

4. using the results of one analysis approach (e.g., initial interviews and/or content analysis of texts) as a starting point for designing further steps (e.g., instrument development) or collecting new data using another approach. For example, many survey questionnaires are constructed after an initial QUAL study in the appropriate population.

Although we do not consider the list of strategies to be comprehensive, it covers a large variety of studies in the social and behavioral sciences. The following sections present examples of these mixed strategies. A slightly different method of classifying these strategies (Caracelli & Greene, 1993) is also presented in Box 6.1.

Concurrent Mixed Data Analysis

(1) Parallel mixed analysis. Also known as triangulation of data sources, parallel analysis of QUAL and QUAN data is probably the most widely used mixed data analysis strategy in the social and behavioral sciences. Many investigators collect a combination of QUAL *and* QUAN data in their studies. In laboratory experiments, the participants are interviewed at the end (postexperimental interview) to determine the type of interpretations and perceptions they had that could have affected their responses. Observation of the participants during the experiment is also a source of data in experiments. While the obtained QUAN data are analyzed through statistical procedures, the interview and observational data are (or can be) analyzed through content analysis.

In survey research, there often is a combination of open-ended and closed-ended response options (see Chapter 4). These closed-ended responses are analyzed statistically, and the open-ended responses are content analyzed. In highly unstructured *qualitative surveys* and *field studies* (see Babbie, 1996), although the bulk of data are qualitative and are analyzed accordingly, there are variables that are (or can be) analyzed quantitatively. The simplest form of such QUAN analysis is to calculate descriptive statistics for the appropriate variables (see Gall et al., 1996, pp. 168-171, for examples).

Similar types of parallel data collection/analysis might be found in most other types of research. It is a hallmark of much educational research in which QUAN data (e.g., tests, formal measures of teachers' classroom behaviors) are collected and analyzed concurrently with QUAL data (e.g., informal school observations or principal and faculty interviews).

(2) Concurrent analysis of the same QUAL data with two methods. This involves the transformation of the QUAL data to a numerical form. Earlier we referred to this transformation as *quantitizing* the QUAL data. Quantitizing might include a simple frequency count of certain themes, responses, behaviors, or events. On the other hand, it may consist of a more complex rating of the strength or intensity of these events, behaviors, or expressions. Depending on the type of transformation, different QUAN techniques might be used for their analysis. For

---

BOX 6.2
An Example of Statistical Analysis
of Qualitative Data

Roberts and Le-Dorze (1994) used a qualitative data collection technique in a study of verbal fluency in patients having aphasia. The data collected were analyzed using both qualitative and quantitative methods. The study's purpose was to explore the verbal fluency of patients with aphasia in ways previous research had not. Data were collected through individual interviews of two groups of aphasia patients: those with recent aphasia and those with chronic aphasia. The interview consisted of a verbal fluency test in which the patient named as many words as possible that would be part of the category requested. Two interviews six to eight weeks apart were conducted with each patient. Quantitative data analysis involved the use of analysis of variance (ANOVA) with group and the number of visits as the independent variables and the total correct score as the dependent variable. Qualitative analysis involved categorizing errors by type and determining the existence of semantic and formal associations within the responses. These data were then quantitized so that statistical analysis could be done. The quantitative analysis showed a main effect for group as the recent group had fewer correct words and a main effect for visit as both groups did better on the second visit but no interaction effect was found. Analysis of the quantitized data showed two interesting results. First, unlike previous research, for both groups there was a significant negative correlation between the number of correct words and the number of errors. Second, a significant correlation was found between the number of semantic associations and the total correct words.

---

example, descriptive statistics might be used to summarize/organize the frequency counts, or more complex procedures such as factor, correlation, or regression analysis might be performed on the ratings. An example of this type of conversion is presented in Box 6.2. The Rusbult, Onizuka, and Lipkus (1993) study presented in Chapter 8 is another example.

(3) Concurrent analysis of the same QUAN data with two methods. This involves the transformation of the QUAN data to QUAL categories, or narrative. Earlier we referred to this transformation as *qualitizing* the QUAN data. An example of such transformation is found in the Hooper (1994) study regarding the effects of language arts tasks in multicultural classrooms (Box 6.3).

BOX 6.3
An Example of Qualitizing
the Quantitative Data

Hooper (1994) conducted a study on the effects of simple and complex literacy language arts tasks on motivation and learning in multiability, multicultural classrooms. Although the study was based on theory and previous research, the study's purpose was exploratory. The main objective of the study was to examine which types of tasks promote intrinsic motivation. Quantitative and qualitative methods were used in the selection of classrooms for the study. The classrooms were selected based on three criteria: range of ability, overall distribution of tasks, and range of language arts and reading subjects. Upon the selection of the pool of classrooms, three groups of students were randomly selected: average ability students from third and fourth grade, sixth grade students with various abilities, and learning disabled students from third grade through sixth grade.

The data were collected with both qualitative and quantitative methods. Each student was interviewed about his or her understanding, expectations, and values regarding two simple and two complex tasks. Some questions involved verbal responses, which made up the qualitative data. Other questions involved answers to questions using a rating scale, which made up the quantitative data. The quantitative data were transformed into qualitative data by assigning a category to each range of scores. The analysis was done at the group level as well as at the individual level. At the group level, analysis involved coding by crossing the level of student's interest with motivation foci. At the individual level, analysis involved crossing task type, literacy response, and reasons for learning. The study found that as language arts and reading tasks move from simple to complex, motivation moves toward intrinsic reasons. The study also raised the possibility that grade level, gender, race, SES, and ability grouping may not be as influential on motivation as once thought.

Qualitizing techniques also include *narrative profile formation.* During the qualitizing process, the investigator constructs verbal descriptions of the individuals under investigation. At least five interrelated types of profiles might be constructed from QUAN (or combined QUAL and QUAN) data. These profile types (modal, average, holistic, comparative, normative) are not mutually exclusive (i.e., their results may be overlapping in some applications). Hence narrative profiles are, at least in some respects, similar to *typology development,* which is discussed in a separate section below. Please note that profiles are the *result* of the concurrent analysis while *typologies* are formed as one step in a sequential analysis (see below).

A description of the five types of profiles follows:

Modal profile. This is a detailed narrative description of a group of people (e.g., a group of women) based on the most frequently occurring attributes in the group. For example, if the majority of individuals are 50 years old, the group is identified as middle-aged.

Average profile. This is a narrative profile based on the average (e.g., mean) of a number of attributes of the individuals or situations. The profile consists of a detailed narrative description of the group on the basis of these average attributes.

Holistic (inferential, summative) profile. This type of narrative profile consists of the overall impressions of the investigator regarding the unit of investigation. Unlike the average profile, the specific information that is the basis of such holistic impressions may not be presented or available.

As was mentioned above, different types of profiles might be mixed. For example, a profile might be based on the most frequent attributes, some averages, and final overall (holistic) inferences regarding a group. A study by Tashakkori, Boyd, and Sines (1996) might be considered an example. The data of their study came from the National Education Longitudinal Study of Eighth Grade (NELS-88; Ingles et al., 1992). The Hispanic eighth graders who dropped out of school between eighth and tenth grade were identified in this national sample. A variety of attitudinal, achievement, family background, and other data were available about each member of this group. Based on these data, profiles were constructed separately for male and female dropout Hispanic youth. These profiles were based on the most frequent type of characteristics in each of the two groups, average scores (for example, self-perception and self-efficacy scores), and overall inferences on the basis of data and the literature.

Comparative profile. This type of narrative profile is the result of comparison of one unit of analysis with another and includes possible differences and/or similarities between them. For example, in a study by Fals-Stewart, Birchler, Schafer, and Lucente (1994), among 102 couples seeking marital therapy, five distinct "types" of couples were identified. The distinction between these "types" was made on the basis of comparing their scores on the Minnesota Multiphasic Personality Inventory (MMPI), a clinical/personality test. Quantitative analysis (cluster analysis) was performed to identify those couples who were similar to each other and different from other couple groups. The five obtained groups were labeled as conflicted, depressed, dissatisfied wives, dysphoric, and domestic calm. These five types were also obtained in a replication sample.

After identifying these groups, a verbal profile of each group was constructed. For example, a description of the "depressed type" is as follows:

> [This group] consisted of partners who were generally anxious, worried, and pessimistic in their general outlook at the time of the testing. These individuals show a narrowing of interests, low frustration tolerance, poor morale, and generally are lacking in self-confidence. Compared to the other clusters (except Cluster 5), these couples do not have many areas of disagreement, nor do they engage excessively in maladaptive responses to conflict. Nevertheless, these couples are reporting a relatively high level of marital dissatisfaction. (p. 235)

Normative profile. These narrative profiles are similar to comparative profiles but are based on the comparison of an individual or group with a standard. The "standard" might be a standardization sample or a specific population. This type of profile is quite common in clinical and personality psychology, psychiatry, and similar disciplines. General impressions and/or narrative descriptions are constructed on the basis of an individual's scores on diagnostic or personality tests such as the MMPI. These impressions are based on comparing the individual's score pattern with that of the normative group.

An example of a normative profile is found in a study by Wetzler, Marlowe, and Sanderson (1994) in which a number of clinical/personality inventories were administered to a group of depressed patients. Each patient was identified with "code types" resulting from comparison of their test scores with the norms for each test (MMPI versus Millon). Narrative profiles of these types were then constructed. For example, the "incapacitated depressive" type on the MMPI was presented as follows:

> [They] are confused, ineffective, and unable to see solutions to problems. They have impaired memory and concentration. They are sensitive to

rejection and keep an emotional distance from others but are equally alienated and disconnected from their own feelings and reactions. As a result, they are difficult to engage in a therapeutic alliance. Psychotherapy should be aimed at labeling their affect—identifying the interpersonal demands of various situations, and advising how they might best respond. (p. 762)

Although profiles are easy to understand and communicate, and provide pictures of "typical" units of analysis, they should be used with caution. Even when they are based on a relatively large number of variables, they might still present an oversimplified view of the group. Also, most profiles assume group homogeneity by taking modal and/or average responses and/or information. Finally, in the formation of profiles, the investigators' subjective analysis might affect the results. This is specifically true regarding holistic profiles in which the investigator's impressions constitute the main basis of description. If a profile is an overall qualitized summary of many detailed quantitative pieces of information, and is also used in conjunction with other quantitative and qualitative data, the dangers of such bias are reduced. As noted in Chapter 2, constructivists consider such bias to be an inevitable feature of the interpretation of qualitative (or any other kind of) data.

Sequential QUAL-QUAN Analysis

In this type of data analysis strategy, an initial QUAL data analysis leads to the identification of groups of individuals who are similar to each other in some respect. These identified groups are then compared either on the QUAN data that are available or on the data that are collected following the QUAL analysis. Some of the variations of this type of sequential strategy follow:

The first is *forming groups of people/settings* on the basis of QUAL data/observations and comparing the groups on QUAN data. Following Caracelli and Greene (1993), presented in Box 6.1, we call this *typology development.* In typology development, individuals are first classified into different types. These groups are then statistically compared with each other on *other* available QUAN (or quantitized) data.

For example, teachers might be categorized into effective and ineffective groups on the basis of field notes taken during observations in their classrooms. The two groups of teachers might be compared on QUAN variables/measures, such as their responses to survey instruments or their students' performance on tests. Comparisons might be performed through univariate or multivariate analysis of variance or covariance, discriminant function analysis, or other statistical techniques. The result of the discriminant function analysis, for example, is the identification of variables that "discriminate" the groups (e.g., effective and ineffective teachers), along with some statistical indicators that show which of these variables discriminates the groups from each other the best.

Advanced nonparametric techniques are also available for comparing the groups. For example, for a two-group case, one might use logistic regression with group membership as the "dependent" or "predicted" variable. The "predictors" might consist of categorical and continuous variables. The result of the analysis is the identification of variables that distinguish the two groups (i.e., predict group membership) the best. Comparable techniques are also available for more than two groups.

The second is forming groups of attributes/themes through content analysis followed by confirmatory statistical analysis of QUAN data that are collected (or are available). As an example, the constant comparative analysis is first used to construct emerging themes from the QUAL data. Categories of themes, variables, or situations that "fit together" (and are distinctly different from other categories) are formed *(construct identification)*. In the next step the QUAN data (either subsequently collected or already available) are statistically analyzed either to confirm or to expand the inferences obtained from the initial QUAL analysis *(construct validation)*.

An example is the classification of teacher's statements (obtained from focus groups) into themes that represent different aspects of a "good principal." The emerging themes or categories are indicators of subconstructs that are parts of the general construct of "principal effectiveness." These categories are formed on the basis of similarities (and/or differences) between teachers' perceptions and beliefs. Survey instruments may then be constructed that include these groups of themes or beliefs and are administered to a group of teachers. The obtained QUAN data may then be factor analyzed to determine the degree of validity of the initial QUAL categories.

An example of this type of strategy is a study by Iwanicki and Tashakkori (1994) in which the "proficiencies of effective principals" that had been obtained though content analysis of QUAL data were measured again through a survey instrument sent to school principals. The data were then subjected to confirmatory factor analysis. Much of the initial typology of proficiencies was confirmed in the QUAN study. Two of the proficiencies were moved from one category to another, and subcategories of these proficiencies were refined further on the basis of the QUAN analysis.

Sequential QUAN-QUAL Analysis

Forming groups of people/settings on the initial basis of QUAN data and then comparing the groups on QUAL data (subsequently collected or available) is similar to the previously discussed sequential QUAL-QUAN analysis. An example of typology development using the sequential QUAN-QUAL analysis may be a study in which an initial QUAN analysis is conducted on data derived from the administration of a survey measuring teachers' perceived efficacy and locus of control. Teachers may be divided into four groups based on the QUAN analysis of their responses to the surveys (i.e., a high- versus low-efficacy classification crossed by internal versus external locus of causality for student success). The four groups of teachers may then be observed and compared on the obtained QUAL data (see Taylor & Tashakkori, 1997, for an example).

The most widely used example of sequential QUAN-QUAL analysis is the qualitative follow-up of individuals/units that are initially identified on the basis of their *residual scores* from multiple regression or their *covariate-adjusted scores* from analysis of covariance (ANCOVA). Detailed QUAL data are then collected on these individuals/units in a search for possible factors that led to their initial high (or low) QUAN scores. The qualitative data are either analyzed through content analysis or are converted to quantitative data for further statistical analysis.

An example of this sequence of analyses involves the initial classification of schools into effective and ineffective categories on the basis of standardized tests using regression residuals (e.g., Kochan, Tashakkori, & Teddlie, 1996). These two types of schools were then observed and compared with each other to explore possible differences between them on other dimensions such as school climate.

Forming categories of attributes/themes through QUAN analysis, and then confirming these categories with the QUAL analysis of other data, is similar to the *construct identification* and *construct validation* procedures described previously. In this strategy, the objective is first to identify the components of a construct (subconstructs) through factor analysis of QUAN data and then to collect QUAL data to validate the categories or to expand upon the information that is available regarding these subconstructs. An example of such mixed data analysis might involve the initial classification of dimensions of teachers' perceptions of school climate through factor analysis of survey data from a sample of faculties. Observational and/or other types of data (e.g., focus group interviews) might then be used to confirm the existence of such dimensions and/or to explore the degree to which these different dimensions are present in everyday interactions.

Caracelli and Greene (1993) discuss another application of this type of analysis. Unlike the above examples, in this application the objective is *not* to confirm or expand the results of construct validation efforts. Instead, the objective is to develop an initial framework for the qualitative/categorical analysis that follows as the next step. For example, factor analytic results might be used as a starting point for the *constant comparative analysis* defined earlier in this chapter. The categories of events/observations that are obtained through factor analysis might then be used for coding the initial qualitative data in the subsequent constant comparative analysis.

Part III

Applications, Examples, and Future Directions of Mixed Model Research

In this section of the book, we present detailed examples of current/ published research using mixed approaches. In Chapter 7, after presenting two summary examples from the literature (Women's Studies Project from Ulin et al., 1996; Patton, 1990), we first discuss confirmatory types of studies. These are studies in which at least some type of tentative conceptual prediction or expectation is possible. We then present examples of exploratory studies. These studies are the ones in which prior predictions were not possible. As stated by Dooley (1995), this is the type of research in which "the data lead to the hypotheses. We may then test such post hoc hypotheses in the usual confirmatory way" (p. 264).

Chapter 8 contains the description of three completely mixed investigations, including a complete example of a longitudinal study that used all of the eight pure and mixed designs presented in Table 3.1. We present these detailed examples to demonstrate the breadth of information that can be collected through complex mixed model designs.

Chapter 9 contains conclusions that we have derived from our examination of mixed methods and mixed models in the social and behavioral sciences. Additionally, this chapter contains speculations regarding future issues related to these mixed methods and models.

7

Examples of Mixed Model Designs

As we discussed in Chapter 3, mixed model Types I through IV are different from Patton's (1990) prototype designs in that instead of differentiating designs as experimental versus naturalistic, we differentiate them according to their degree of being confirmatory (including qualitative case studies, experimental designs, and nonexperimental studies) versus exploratory (including naturalistic inquiry as well as quantitative exploratory studies such as surveys). Some examples of these designs are presented below and also in the next chapter.

Please note that the Patton examples presented in Box 7.1 are specific cases of our mixed model design Types I, II, III, and IV, as follows:

Type I: Confirmatory investigation, qualitative data, statistical analysis (form 2 in Box 7.1)

Type II: Confirmatory investigation, qualitative data, qualitative analysis (form 1 in Box 7.1)

Type III: Exploratory investigation, quantitative data, statistical analysis (form 4 in Box 7.1)

Type IV: Exploratory investigation, qualitative data, statistical analysis (form 3 in Box 7.1)

Patton did not include examples of Types V and VI designs because they are rare, involving qualitizing techniques (see Chapter 6).

CONFIRMATORY INVESTIGATIONS

The mixed model confirmatory designs were noted in Table 3.1 as mixed model designs Types I, II, and V. Historically, in confirmatory studies, the data primarily have been quantitative, the conceptual framework has been deductive, and the data analysis has been statistical. However, in the mixed confirmatory designs discussed here, the data can be qualitative or quantitative and can be analyzed in either form as well. At least tentative

BOX 7.1
Examples of "Mixed Forms" of
Evaluation Research From Patton

These are possible projects to evaluate a program serving high-risk students who were likely to be involved with the criminal justice system.

(1) Mixed form: Experimental design, qualitative data, and content analysis. As in the pure experimental form, potential participants are randomly assigned to treatment and control groups. In-depth interviews are conducted with all youth, both those in the treatment group and those in the control group, before the program begins. The focus of those interviews is similar to that in the pure qualitative approach. Interviews are conducted again at the end of the program. Content analysis is performed separately on the data from the control group and the experimental group. The patterns found in the control group and the experimental group are then compared and contrasted.

(2) Mixed form: Experimental design, qualitative data, and statistical analysis. Participants are randomly assigned to treatment and control groups, and in-depth interviews are conducted both before the program and at the end of the program. These interview data, in raw form, are then given to a panel of judges who rate each interview along several outcome dimensions operationalized as a ten-point scale.

For both the "pre" interview and the "post" interview, the judges assign ratings on such dimensions as likelihood of success in school (low = 1, high = 10), likelihood of committing criminal offenses (low = 1, high = 10), commitment to education, commitment to engaging in productive work, self-esteem, and manifestation of desired nutritional and health habits. Inferential statistics are then used to compare these two groups. Judges make the ratings without knowledge of which participants were in which group. Outcomes on the rated scales are also statistically related to background characteristics of participants.

(3) Mixed form: Naturalistic inquiry, qualitative data, statistical analysis. As in the pure qualitative form, students are selected for the program on the basis of whatever criteria staff choose to apply. In-depth interviews are conducted with all students before the program and at the end of the program. These data are then submitted to a panel of judges, who rate them on a series of dimensions similar to those listed in the previous example. Change scores are computed for each individual, and changes are statistically related to background characteristics of the students to determine in a regression format which characteristics of students are likely to predict success in the program. In addition, observations of program activities are

(continued)

rated on a set of scales developed to quantify the climate attributes of activities: for example, the extent to which the activity involved active or passive participation, the extent to which student-teacher interaction was high or low, the extent to which interactions were formal or informal, and the extent to which participants had input into program activities. Ratings of activities based on qualitative descriptions are then aggregated to provide an overview of the treatment environment of the program.

(4) Mixed form: Naturalistic inquiry, quantitative data, statistical analysis. Students are selected for the program according to staff criteria. The evaluator enters the program setting without any predetermined categories of analysis or presuppositions about important variables or variable relationships. The evaluator observes important activities and events in the program, looking for the types of behaviors and interactions that will emerge. For each new type of behavior or interaction, the evaluator creates a category and then uses a time and space sampling design to count the frequency with which those categories of behavior and interaction are exhibited. The frequency of the manifestation of observed behaviors and interactions is then statistically related to such characteristics as group size, duration of the activity, staff-student ratios, and social/physical density.

SOURCE: Patton (1990, pp. 191-193).

NOTE: These are possible projects to evaluate a program serving high-risk students who were likely to be involved with the criminal justice system.

predictions are made and tested in investigations using these designs. The following sections address the three types of designs in this group.

Type I: Confirmatory investigation, qualitative data and operations, statistical analysis and inference

In this type of study, the collected data are qualitative; they are quantitized and then subjected to statistical analysis. This is one of the most frequently used mixed designs in the literature. The Pemberton, Insko, and Schopler (1996) study of group versus individual competitiveness is an example of this design. An initial experiment (see Pemberton et al., 1996, p. 954, for details) had demonstrated that college students recalled more competitive intergroup interactions than interindividual interactions. Following that experiment, the authors asked questions regarding the reasons that intergroup interaction was perceived as more competitive. Tentative answers were suggested on the basis of theory and previous research: (a) awareness of experimental expectations (discussed in Chapters 4 and 5 under *participant reactivity* or *participant roles*), (b) existence of an out-group schema, and (c) memory effects (previous group experiences have been in sports, where competition is the norm).

In the Type I study that followed, Pemberton and his colleagues used the *Rochester Interaction Record* (RIR; Reis & Wheeler, 1991) data collection procedures to record interactions in the natural environment. A number of hypotheses/predictions were formulated and tested; for example, it was predicted that participants would recall more competitive group events. Also, it was predicted that observation of actual events recorded through the RIR would show greater competitiveness in intergroup interactions than in interindividual ones.

The participants were 28 male and 27 female introductory psychology students. As a part of the RIR procedures, each participant was given a booklet containing 40 sheets, one sheet for recording each interaction. Each participant was asked to record the date and circle the type of interaction that occurred (e.g., one-on-one, one-on-group, group-on-one, and group-on-group).

An interesting characteristic of this experiment was that the participants were used as raters for quantitizing the qualitative data (interactions). Each recorded event was rated on a 7-point scale at the time of recording (as soon as the participants recorded the event). The ratings pertained to the perceived degree of competitiveness or cooperativeness of the interaction. These quantitized data were then statistically analyzed and reported.

The Smith, Sells, and Clevenger (1994) study is another example of this type of design. During an investigation on reflecting team practice in marriage counseling, they collected qualitative data, quantitized parts of them, and analyzed them quantitatively using chi-square and the phi correlation coefficient. Box 7.2 presents a summary of that study.

Type II: Confirmatory investigation, qualitative data and operations, qualitative analysis and inference

This mixed design is basically a confirmatory qualitative study. In contrast to the traditional naturalistic design, these investigations use tentative predictions in at least some aspects of the research. The most common studies in this group are the ones that use qualitative data collection and analysis to confirm or disconfirm (triangulate) the findings from a previous study.

Sinclair's (1994) study is an example of an investigation in which this type of design was the dominant mode. Sinclair used qualitative data and

---

BOX 7.2
An Example of Type I Mixed Model Study

The Smith et al. (1994) study was a confirmatory investigation involving unstructured interviews with couples who participated in marital therapy sessions. In a previous study, they had collected qualitative data consisting of interviews of couples in therapy and their therapists. Qualitative analysis of the data led to two themes. First, the therapists and the couples' perceptions differed with regard to reflecting team practice. Second, these differences were associated "with the spatial distance or boundary" between the couples and the "client-index therapist system" (p. 269). The purpose of the current study was to confirm hypotheses based on these two assertions.

Qualitative data were collected through ethnographic interviews of couples and therapists during a four-month period. The categories of the previous study were used in the initial qualitative analysis of the data. Content analysis led to the refinement of seven categories. Frequency of occurrence for each of these categories of themes/perceptions was recorded and quantitatively analyzed.

For the first hypothesis, chi-square was used to compare the frequency of each category between the couples' and the therapists' perceptions. Results showed that both groups discussed gender with the same frequency. Although the therapists were most concerned with the use of reflecting team practice in the sessions, the couples were most concerned with the benefits of the practice. Phi correlation between the co-occurrence of "Spatial Separateness" and "Process of Hearing" was calculated to test the second hypothesis. A strong correlation was found between these two. "These co-occurrences of spacial separateness and process of hearing were supported by many examples throughout the text" (p. 280).

---

procedures to test four hypotheses regarding the effects of prediction making as an instructional method in science classrooms. Participating students were divided into two groups: an experimental group that used prediction-making activities as part of a genetics unit and a control group that was taught a genetics unit in a traditional manner. Qualitative data collection involved student interviews, teacher interviews, teacher logs, and classroom observations. Qualitative analysis consisted of the use of Bogdan and Biklen's (1982) constant comparative method in which responses were put into categories.

Qualitative analysis showed that prediction activities led to greater student involvement and interest in class. Students in the experimental group participated more in class, asked more "thoughtful" questions, and seemed to enjoy the classes more than those in the control group. The observers reported greater "give-and-take" dialogues between the students and the teachers in these classes than in the control group. Qualitative analysis also revealed that differences in the teaching styles of the teachers affected the way the classes in both groups were conducted, and probably affected the results of the study.

Another example of this type of design is a study by Mann (1994) in which qualitative data were collected regarding two groups of tutors. One group consisted of three tutors who seemed to have benefitted the most from a training program (they had the highest scores on outcome measures). The control group consisted of those tutors who had not benefitted from the training program (had low scores on the outcome measures). The general hypothesis was that the two groups of tutors would be different in their conceptualization of their role as well as their effects on the tutee.

Qualitative data collection involved weekly journal entries during a 10-week period and a two-page essay written by each tutor. Qualitative analysis of the journal entries showed that the tutors with high scores were more aware of the interpersonal aspects of tutoring, identified conflicts in clearer forms, and resolved them more efficiently than the low-scoring group. The low-score tutors were more preoccupied with evaluating the sessions and with overgeneralizing the problems of the tutee. They experienced more anxiety and less success than the high-score tutors. (For detailed verbal examples of these journal entries, see Mann, 1994.)

Type V: Confirmatory investigation, quantitative data and operations, qualitative analysis and inference

Although this type of design is rare, examples are sprinkled throughout the literature in several fields of study. The quantitative data are qualitized and presented/analyzed qualitatively.

Typical Type V studies identify and present verbal "profiles" for groups and/or individuals on the basis of quantitative data. An example of this kind of study might be an investigation designed to identify the attributes of different groups or "types" of female contraceptive users in an urban center in Zaire on the basis of interview (survey) data. The typology is developed on the basis of previous research (for example, consistent user, sporadic user) but a holistic profile (see Chapter 6) is developed for each type or group on the basis of survey data. See examples of this type of design in Chapter 8.

EXPLORATORY STUDIES

The mixed model exploratory designs were noted in Table 3.1 as mixed model designs Types III, IV, and VI. These mixed model exploratory studies might use qualitative or quantitative data and analyze them using either of the two approaches. The following sections present three different types of designs in this group.

Type III: Exploratory investigation, quantitative data and operations, statistical analysis and inference

This type of design is actually the same as traditional quantitative exploratory investigations (usually known as descriptive studies) in which no predictions were made beforehand. The reason for inclusion of these studies as mixed model studies is that they do not fit in the traditional hypothetico-deductive type of investigation using the logical schemata that we presented in Table 3.1. This parallel between traditional descriptive and mixed Type III designs is a good example of a phenomenon that will be expanded upon in Chapter 9: Researchers working in traditional areas (e.g., psychology, anthropology, sociology) may be using mixed model designs but may be so ingrained in the QUAN or the QUAL tradition that they believe they are doing "pure" QUAN or QUAL research.

A recent exploratory study by Aghajanian and Moghadas (in press) is an example of a Type III design. They investigated recent divorce trends in Iran, including potential determinants and consequences of these patterns. As is common in exploratory studies, they had no a priori hypotheses. The data were collected through a survey study in a large urban center. A multilevel sample of married and divorced women was selected on the basis of the 1986 census. In the first stage, 43 census districts were randomly selected from 169. All households that had at least one divorced woman were identified in the census data. The result was a sample of 254 women who had been married once and divorced once. A comparison (2% random) sample was also selected consisting of women who were currently married and never divorced. Female interviewers visited each household and interviewed the identified woman. Detailed data were collected regarding socioeconomic characteristics, attitudes, health, and problems.

The results suggested that the divorce rate has evolved in response to social and legal changes and several years of war with Iraq. The main differentiators between the two groups of women (divorced, not divorced)

were found to be urbanicity, education, work status, and religiosity. A greater proportion of divorced women were from urban centers, had either low or high education (as compared with a middle level), and were less religious. Regarding the consequences of divorce, divorced women were found to suffer economically and experience more psychological problems than nondivorced women. Also, the children of divorced women experienced higher levels of emotional problems and delinquency than those of nondivorced women. It was concluded than the consequences of divorce in Iran are much more severe than those found in the United States. Also, the inverse relationship between the age of first marriage and probability of divorce that is reported in the United States was not found in Iran.

Type IV: Exploratory investigation, qualitative data and operations, statistical analysis and inference

A large number of studies have used projective techniques (sentence completion, stories, and so on) for collecting data in psychological and sociological research. After collection, the data are quantitized (see Chapter 6) through different procedures and analyzed through (mostly nonparametric) techniques such as log-linear modeling and logistic regression.

Type VI: Exploratory investigation, quantitative data and operations, qualitative analysis and inference

This is another relatively rare design in which quantitative data are collected and subjected to qualitative analysis and presentation. The discussion of qualitizing the quantitative data presented in Chapter 6 included examples of this type of design. In such studies, groups of participants are formed (e.g., extreme-case groups, types of participants) on the basis of the quantitative information. These groups are then described in qualitative (narrative) form (e.g., what we called "profile formation" in Chapter 6).

The Rusbult et al. (1993) study (discussed in detail in Chapter 8) is an example of Type VI mixed model studies. In this exploratory study, participants were asked to rate a set of descriptions regarding romantic relationships. These descriptions were rated with regard to their degree of similarity to a set of "target" descriptions. Based on multidimensional scaling analysis (a multivariate statistical analysis), four types of relationships were identified in these descriptions. These four prototypes were then described in detail on the basis of both qualitative and quantitative information. Box 7.3 presents two examples of these prototypes (profiles).

BOX 7.3
Examples of the Different Prototypes (Profiles)
in the Rusbult et al. Study

Picturebook fantasy (female): "Quadrant 1 mental models received low ratings for Intimacy and high ratings for Romance-Traditionalism and were highly idealized, developed quickly and spontaneously, included explicit requirements for involvement, were not egalitarian (e.g., traditional sex roles were common), de-emphasized friendship, were not based on respect/admiration, and tended to be male initiated. Rather than seeking trust and intimacy, these subjects yearned for the classic romantic fantasy—glamorous activities, an exciting life, and passion. Love at first sight was a common theme. These ideals are termed Picturebook Fantasy and are illustrated by the following excerpts: It would be love at first sight. My partner would have an endless number of good qualities. He would never pressure me sexually—he would be very mature about it, unlike most guys. . . . I would be in love almost to the point of obsession, and I would never before have felt so happy.

Companionship (male): "Quadrant 4 mental models were the mirror image of those in Quadrant 1 and were characterized by slow development, egalitarianism, friendship orientation, a practical orientation to living with the partner, high respect/admiration, the absence of male initiation, and few explicit requirements for the relationship. This is a very comfortable, low-key ideal—partners are buddies and allies, sharing career interests and political beliefs and life concerns. The following excerpts illustrate Quadrant 4 Companionship: It would revolve around trust and mutuality. We'd be "up front" with each other—I don't enjoy playing games. Honesty would be very important. Also, I like a girl who is aggressive, I don't like to do all the work and take all the risks. . . . She'd be able to talk to other men and I wouldn't feel jealous or "inadequate." She'd love me for what I am, not for what I have or who I associate with or what fraternity I belong to.

SOURCE: Rusbult et al. (1993, pp. 507-509).

Another example of this type of design is a study by Taylor and Tashakkori (1997) discussed in Chapter 8. The authors collected survey data from a sample of teachers in a restructured school district. The researchers had no a priori hypotheses. Two specific types of questions were included in these surveys: regarding teachers' desire/motivation for participation in decision making and their reports of actual involvement in decisions regarding instructional and school issues. Four extreme groups of teachers were formed on the basis of their scores on these two dimensions (desire for participation versus actual participation). The result was the identification of four "types" of teachers in this two-dimensional model. These four types were labeled "empowered" (those who wanted to participate and did), "disenfranchised" (those who wanted to participate but did not), "involved" (those who did not want to participate but were involved in decision making), and "disengaged" (those who did not want to participate and did not). Verbal (qualitative) modal profiles were constructed on the basis of other information that was available about each group of teachers.

8

Extended Examples of Mixed Model Designs

As we discussed before, completely mixed investigations simultaneously use both types of data collection (qualitative and quantitative) and both types of data analysis (statistical *and* qualitative analysis). Some may also combine the exploratory approach with a confirmatory research study. Box 8.1 presents a graphic illustration of mixed model strategies that were used in a large-scale international study of women's reproductive health (Ulin et al., 1996). As the illustration shows, the degree and type of mixing may vary across subprojects of this large-scale study.

We present three extended examples of completely mixed investigations in this chapter. The ultimate goal of the chapter is to provide graduate students and interested researchers with more concrete examples of completely mixed studies that can be used as models.

In Table 1.1, we referred to these types of studies as mixed model studies with multiple applications within each stage of research (type of inquiry, or data collection/operations, or analysis/inference). A note to the table further explained that mixing must occur such that both approaches appear in at least one stage of the study. The examples in this chapter have mixing at both the data collection/operation *and* the analysis/inference stages.

The first extended example (Taylor & Tashakkori, 1997; Taylor, Tashakkori, & Hardwick, 1996) is a *parallel mixed model* study: It combined QUAL and QUAN data collection, data analysis, and an inference process in a parallel form (multiple simultaneous approach). The inference process drifts simultaneously between inductive and deductive, and the data collection and analysis are simultaneously qualitative and quantitative.

The second example (Rusbult et al., 1993) is different in that each phase of the investigation was dependent on the finding, conceptual development, or material that was generated in a previous phase. As such, that study can be more readily considered to be an example of *sequential mixed model* investigations. In these studies, multiple approaches to data collection,

BOX 8.1
A Graphic Illustration of Mixed Model/Design
Research in a Multinational Study

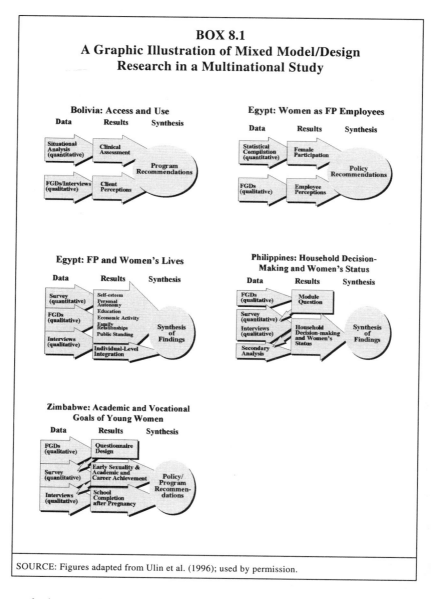

SOURCE: Figures adapted from Ulin et al. (1996); used by permission.

analysis, and inference are employed in a sequence of phases. Each phase, by itself, may use a mixed approach and provide conceptual and/or methodological grounds for the next one in the chain.

Table 8.1

Complex Mixed Model Designs: Types VII and VIII

Type VII: Parallel Mixed Model Studies[*]	Type VIII: Sequential Mixed Model Studies[**]
A One-Phase Study	Phase One of the Study
Stage One:	Stage One:
Type of Inquiry: QUAL and QUAN	Type of Inquiry: QUAL or QUAN
Stage Two:	Stage Two:
Data collection/operations: QUAL and QUAN	Data collection/operations: QUAL or QUAN
Stage Three:	Stage Three:
Analysis/Inference QUAL and QUAN	Analysis/Inference QUAL or QUAN
	Phase Two of the Study
	Stage One:
	Type of Inquiry: QUAL or QUAN
	Stage Two:
	Data collection/operations: QUAL or QUAN
	Stage Three:
	Analysis/Inference QUAL or QUAN
	Other Iterative Phases

*There must be mixing such that both approaches appear in at least one *stage* of the study.
**There must be mixing such that each approach appears in at least one *phase* of the study.

The third extended example presents a long-term project, the Louisiana School Effectiveness Study (LSES; Stringfield & Teddlie, 1990, 1991; Teddlie & Stringfield, 1993; Teddlie et al., 1989), with multiple phases and a variety of combinations of mixed model designs in each. We use this project as a final, detailed, step-by-step example of a mixed model investigation in which each of the eight types of studies described in Table 3.1 (pure and mixed model designs), as well as more complex combinations of these designs, were employed.

Table 8.1 contains an elaboration of parallel mixed model studies (mixed model Type VII) and sequential mixed model studies (mixed model Type VIII). The distinction between stage and phase of a study is made in this table. An example of such a distinction is presented in Table 8.2. A *stage,* as defined in Chapter 1, refers to a component of a study. For example, in most studies, stages are the framing of the research question and the determination of the type of inquiry, data collection, data analysis, and final inferences. *Phase* refers to a complete research effort consisting of a number of stages. Each phase is a part of the overall study. For instance, a research study could have a primarily qualitative phase (consisting of

Table 8.2

Five Phases of the Louisiana School Effectiveness Study

Phase	Brief Description	Period
LSES-I Pilot study	• Conceptualized project in 1980-1981 • Conducted pilot study in 1981-1982, including field test of instruments • Completed LSES-I report	1980-1982
LSES-II Macro-level study (process-product study)	• Selected sample of 76 schools • Collected school climate questionnaires and other instruments from 74 principals, 250 teachers, and more than 5,400 students in 1982-1983 • Analyzed data • LSES-II report completed in 1984	1982-1984
LSES-III Micro-level longitudinal study (case studies, first-round site visits)	• Selected sample of eight matched pairs of schools • Conducted more than 700 hours of classroom observations and more than 1,000 hours of on-site data collection in 1984-1985 • Analyzed data • Prepared research reports and articles using LSES-III quantitative and qualitative data	1984-1988
LSES-IV Micro-level longitudinal study continued (case studies, second-round site visits)	• Designed LSES-IV during 1988-1989 • Conducted more than 650 hours of classroom observations and more than 950 total hours of on-site data collection in 1989-1990 • Analyzed data • Prepared research reports and articles using both LSES-III and IV data sources	1988-1992
LSES-V Micro-level longitudinal study continued (case studies, third-round site visits)	• Published *Schools Make a Difference: Lessons Learned from a 10-Year Study of School Effects*, summarizing LSES-I through LSES-IV in 1993 • Designed LSES-V during 1994-1995 • Conducted more than 500 hours of classroom observations and more than 750 total hours of on-site data collection in 1995-1996 • Began data analysis	1992-1996

design, data collection, data analysis, inference stages) followed by a primarily quantitative phase with comparable stages.

Parallel mixed model studies (Type VII) involve mixing within each phase of the investigation. At least one stage of the study (for example, data collection) involves both QUAL and QUAN approaches. Sequential mixed model studies (Type VIII) involve mixing across phases. Each phase predominantly involves one of the two approaches (either QUAL or QUAN), although some degree of mixing might be present in one or more of its stages. The next phase of the study uses the other approach. For example, if Phase 1 is predominantly QUAL, Phase 2 would predominantly be QUAN. Furthermore, each phase is designed to explore the questions raised in the previous phase, or to confirm it.

AN EXAMPLE OF A PARALLEL
MIXED MODEL STUDY (TYPE VII)

An investigation of school restructuring effects by Taylor et al. (1996; Taylor & Tashakkori, 1997) combined qualitative and quantitative data collection, analysis, and inference processes in the form of a completely mixed study. In that study, all teachers in a school district were asked to respond to a survey instrument with closed-ended questions. The instrument combined selected subscales from the National Educational Longitudinal Study of 1988 with a subscale from an instrument developed by Bacharach, Bauer, and Shedd (1986). Items asked for teachers' perceptions regarding school climate, student discipline, teachers' sense of efficacy, and teachers' participation in decision making. Response choices were arrayed in a four-part Likert format ranging from strongly disagree to strongly agree. An open-ended section was added to collect qualitative responses by asking teachers to share their feelings and opinions about their school and related issues.

In addition to collecting survey data, classroom observations in each of the seven schools were made by trained observers. Observations occurred in at least eight classrooms per school on two different occasions. Extensive field notes recorded not only data from these classroom observations but also details about other aspects of each school. A third component of the research design involved focus groups that were conducted separately with elementary and middle/high school teachers, elementary and middle/high school students, school administrators, school board members, and parents.

Data analysis consisted of both quantitative and qualitative techniques. Univariate and multivariate analyses were conducted on the survey data.

Content analysis was performed on the open-ended responses, field notes, and transcribed focus group interviews. As a part of these analyses, some of the qualitative data were quantitized by counting the frequency of occurrence of events. Also, some of the quantitative data were qualitized by forming groups of teachers on the basis of responses to the survey instruments (see the example in Chapter 7). Brief profiles were constructed for each of these groups. Results were presented both in terms of quantitative indices and in terms of qualitative inferences.

AN EXAMPLE OF A SEQUENTIAL
MIXED MODEL STUDY

Although the investigators did not identify their methodology as "mixed," a study by Rusbult et al. (1993) is an interesting example of such a design. It is an interesting example for at least three reasons: (a) the authors efficiently combined experimental procedures with qualitative data collection and inference; (b) they conducted a set of sequential studies, each using the material and/or conceptual framework obtained in the previous phase; and (c) the study is an example of a research project that could have benefitted from the use of detailed and systematic qualitative content analysis of the qualitative data, such as discussed in Chapter 6.

The study was based on an initial review of the literature, including the social-psychological theories of liking, love, and romantic relationships. The main research question, following these reviews, was as follows: "Do people hold expectations about ideal romantic involvement that are compatible with these theories?" (p. 498). Not finding an answer to this general question in the social-psychological literature, four specific questions were raised to guide the study: (a) What dimensions distinguish among young adults' mental models of ideal involvement (i.e., how do mental models of ideal involvement differ)? (b) What are the primary mental models of ideal involvement? (c) Do stated ideals parallel the ways in which young adults think about actual or potential relationships? (d) Are there substantive differences between men's and women's mental models of ideal involvement?

The investigation started in a descriptive, qualitative, and largely inductive direction. However, as new studies (phases) were added to the investigation, the researchers collected mostly quantitative data and analyzed them statistically. Three studies were conducted to explore the "young adults' mental models of ideal romantic involvement" (p. 493). Each of the first two studies was conducted in three phases.

Phase 1 of the project involved qualitative data, partial qualitative analysis, and development of materials for Phase 2 of the study. Participants (undergraduate students) were asked to describe ideal romantic involvement (qualitative data). The obtained descriptions were edited for grammar and clarity, and each was printed on a small index card. The ratings of multiple judges regarding each expression were solicited and summed to obtain an overall index of the degree of clarity.

From the set of descriptions that were judged to be the most clear (overall clarity score above the median), 50 (25 expressed by men and 25 by women) were selected for the next phase (in a second study, all 35 descriptions were retained). Ten of the descriptions were selected (and were called "targets" in the rest of the report). The participants were asked to judge the degree of similarity of all other descriptors to these 10 "targets."

Phase 2 of the study also involved having qualitative data quantitized by the respondents and analyzed statistically. The respondents were asked to rank order the qualitative descriptors obtained in Phase 1 according to their degree of similarity to a "target" scenario that was assigned to each participant. They were specifically asked to pay attention to the ideal of romantic involvement that was expressed in the description. After ranking the descriptions, each participant was also asked to write a brief summary of the criteria he or she used to distinguish among the descriptions (either these qualitative data were not analyzed, or their qualitative analysis is not reported). Difference scores were calculated between the ranks assigned to each possible pair of descriptions. These "dissimilarity" scores were then subjected to multidimensional scaling (ALSCAL; see Takane, Young, & DeLeeuw, 1977).

Based on different statistical considerations, a two-dimensional model (configuration) was identified to distinguish the difference between the descriptions. One of the two dimensions consisted of intimate versus superficial relationship. The other consisted of a romantic/traditional versus practical/nontraditional type of relationship. Based on this (2×2) configuration, four categories of ideal relationships were identified: picturebook fantasy, marital bliss, utilitarian involvement, and companionship.

The two dimensions of the "mental model" that represent the participants' thoughts about relationships, and the four quadrants that are obtained in such a two-dimensional model, could not be labeled on the basis of statistical analysis. Phase 3 of the investigation was an attempt to obtain qualitative interpretations and/or labels for these dimensions and quadrants. From Phase 2, 39 potential labels were developed for different configurations of relationships. These labels were obtained from several sources: participant's descriptions in Phase 2, investigators' interpretations of the obtained statistical dimensions, and models and theories of romantic love in the social-psychological literature.

The study (in multiple phases) identified the types of romantic relationships and their possible differences. The next research question asked by Rusbult et al. was whether the identified mental models were the result of daydreams or were indeed the same as the actual mental representations that young adults use in evaluating their romantic relationships. A new study was designed to answer this question. Participants in this study were 25 men and 26 women who self-identified themselves as being involved in a dating relationship for at least a month. They were asked to write essays in response to one of three detailed instructional sets describing their (a) ideal romantic relationship, (b) what they look for in a romantic relationship, and (c) their current romantic relationship.

Judges were trained to rate each description with regard to its correspondence to the category labels obtained in Phase 3 of the previous study. For each category, ratings assigned to descriptions were averaged to obtain a single category score. These category scores were then compared across the three scenarios (instructional sets; see above).

Analysis of variance revealed very few differences between the three settings. Also, category labels were divided into four groups corresponding to the four quadrants obtained from earlier (Phase 3) statistical analyses. Correlational analyses were performed to assess the degree of correspondence between the category scores in the four obtained quadrants. Based on these analyses, the authors concluded that the "mental models" that were obtained in the previous study were consistent with the real (actual) ones obtained in the current study.

A STEP-BY-STEP EXAMPLE OF SIMPLE AND COMPLEX MIXED MODEL DESIGNS IN A SINGLE STUDY

The Louisiana School Effectiveness Study was conceived in 1980, and final data collection occurred in spring 1996. During its 16+-year history, the study has progressed through five phases of data collection, interspersed with periods of analysis and report writing. The five phases are summarized in Table 8.2, and the following section will briefly describe the overall design of the study.

The Design of LSES-I and LSES-II

The first and second phases of the LSES (LSES-I and LSES-II) were conducted primarily as confirmatory studies, while the final three phases (LSES-III through LSES-V) included both exploratory and confirmatory components. The LSES was always driven by basic research questions. Specific and innovative research methodologies evolved for answering these questions during the history of the project. The following section on the overall designs of LSES-I through LSES-V was adapted from Teddlie and Stringfield (1993).

The pilot study (LSES-I) was conducted during school year 1981-1982. Two separate activities were accomplished during LSES-I: (a) The school climate questionnaires, modified from those used by Brookover et al. (1979), were field tested in one school district and refined based on the information gained there; and (b) the entire methodology for LSES-II was pilot tested in a number of schools in a second district. In the field test of the modified student school climate questionnaire, the authors first surveyed third grade students in regular classroom settings and then interviewed small groups of students to determine if they understood the questions and to gather information on how the instrument might be improved.

Data for LSES-II were collected during the 1982-1983 school year (Teddlie, Falkowski, Stringfield, Desselle, & Garvue, 1984). The sampling frame for LSES-II was designed to make the study sample representative of the statewide population of elementary schools. Altogether, 76 schools with more than 250 third grade teachers and more than 5,400 third grade students were included in the sample. Twelve school districts participated in LSES-II, including urban, suburban, and rural areas.

The major instruments used in LSES-II were a norm-referenced achievement test (NRT) and the modified Brookover et al. (1979) student, teacher, and principal school climate questionnaires. The student questionnaires were mass administered during regularly scheduled classes, and the principals and teachers completed the instruments on their own. Teams of researchers entered each of the 76 schools and gathered the data in one day. Archived data (e.g., student SES data, results from state-administered criterion-referenced tests, or CRTs, and school structural characteristics) were also collected from several secondary sources.

LSES-II was conceptualized as a large-scale process-product study similar to that conducted by Brookover et al. (1979) in Michigan. The emphases in data analysis were twofold: (a) to determine the amount of variance in student achievement that was attributable to student SES and to measures of school climate and (b) to compare schools that varied in terms of effectiveness status and SES characteristics of student body.

The first set of analyses used both multiple regression and HLM (hierarchical linear modeling) techniques. The second set of analyses (multivariate and univariate analyses of variance or MANOVAs/ANOVAs) enabled the researchers to make the following comparisons: (a) differences among effective, typical, and ineffective schools; (b) differences between middle- and low-SES schools; and (c) differences among the six groups of schools generated by the design.

The Design of LSES-III Through LSES-V

These phases were designed to determine the degree to which individual schools retained their effectiveness status over time despite changes in student body and staffing. These phases were designed to provide longitudinal case studies of eight matched pairs of effective and ineffective schools during an 11-year time period. Schools for these three phases were purposefully selected to represent different geographic regions and urbanicity contexts within the state. The sampling procedure was complex, involving nine separate steps (Teddlie & Stringfield, 1993). Data collection occurred in 1984-1985 (LSES III). The same schools were revisited in 1989-1990 and 1995-1996 during LSES-V.

Numerous instruments were used in the study. They included student, teacher, and principal school climate instruments; NRT achievement tests for all third grade students; protocols for interviewing teachers and principals; a 12-page school observation checklist; high-inference classroom observation instruments (measuring quality of teaching); low-inference classroom observation instruments (measuring time-on-task); an instrument designed to assess school-level climate that was completed by the researchers; and sociometric indices to assess relationships among faculty members. These instruments included a mix of QUAL and QUAN measures.

Observers spent several days in each school during these three phases of the study (12 person days per school in LSES-III, 10 person days in LSES-IV, 10 days in LSES-V). A major focus of LSES-III through LSES-V was the gathering of classroom observational data on teachers in matched pairs of effective and ineffective schools. Therefore, more than 700 hours of classroom observations were recorded in LSES-III, some 650 hours were logged in classrooms in LSES-IV, and 500 hours were spent in the classrooms in LSES-V. The results from these classroom observations constituted a large portion of the results from this part of the study.

In the following sections, we present examples from the LSES of all eight of the pure and mixed research designs described in Table 3.1.

Purely Quantitative Study

LSES-II followed in the tradition of quantitatively oriented educational production function studies conducted in school effectiveness research. One of its major purposes was to determine the proportion of variance in student achievement that was attributable either to family background (e.g., SES of students attending the school, other student body demographic characteristics) or to the influence of the school (e.g., school climate). This portion of the LSES was purely quantitative. The study was confirmatory, with hypotheses set up in advance asserting that the school climate variables would predict a significant proportion of the variance in student achievement, thus proving that "schools make a difference." The data collection and operations were purely quantitative, with the use of paper-and-pencil attitudinal scales, NRT data, and numerical archived data. The analyses and inferences were purely quantitative, using regression or HLM statistical techniques and interpreting the results in light of the study hypotheses and previous research results.

Purely Qualitative Study

The longitudinal case studies (LSES-III through V) were set up with exploratory research questions and confirmatory hypotheses, employed both qualitative and quantitative data and procedures, and used both qualitative data analyses and statistical analyses. Therefore, in general, these case studies are examples of what we call "completely mixed investigations" or "multiple applications within stage of study" mixed models in Table 1.1.

While the case studies were completely mixed investigations, there were independent studies within them that were purely qualitative in nature. The best example of a purely qualitative design within the LSES was the "naturally occurring school improvement" study from LSES-III reported by Stringfield and Teddlie (1990). In this study, the researchers "discovered" a phenomenon that had not been discussed in school effectiveness research: Some schools previously designated and confirmed as ineffective schools were improving, without any external change agent being involved. The initial data collection and operations for this portion of the LSES were purely qualitative, based on narrative data obtained through field notes, interviews, observations, and audiotapes. The analyses and inferences were purely qualitative, using the inductive reasoning process solely and the constant comparative technique in particular. Themes related to the process of "naturally occurring school improvement" emerged as a result of these qualitative analyses.

Type I Mixed Study: Confirmatory Investigation, Qualitative Data/Operations, Statistical Analysis and Inference

The research reported by Teddlie et al. (1989) is an example from LSES-III of a Type I mixed design in which the authors of a confirmatory study used the *quantitizing* methodology described in Chapter 6. Open-ended results from the Classroom Observation Instrument (COI) were converted to numerical data, which were then analyzed using *t*-tests and MANOVAs/ANOVAs. The researchers set out to determine if different types of classroom teaching behavior occurred in differentially effective schools. They predicted that more effective schools would be characterized by teachers who provided higher quality instruction than teachers in less effective schools. Teacher quality was measured by the Stallings's Classroom Snapshot (Stallings, 1980; Stallings & Kaskowitz, 1974), which resulted in numerical indices of time-on-task, and the COI.

The COI was developed to provide high-inference classroom data in the form of field notes regarding 15 general indicators of teacher effectiveness. These indicators were based on characteristics of effective teaching gleaned from reviews by Rosenshine (1983) and Rosenshine and Stevens (1986) and included measures of time-on-task, initial student practice, presentation of new material, and positive reinforcement. Specific cues associated with "initial student practice" included a high frequency of questions, teacher-directed exchange, teacher prompts, opportunity for all students to respond, and success rates of 80% during initial student practice. Observers were directed to complete field notes in each of the 15 categories as behavior associated with that category occurred in the classroom being observed.

During LSES-III, observers coded teaching and student behaviors in 700 separate classes. Altogether, more than 25,000 units of information were recorded (700 classes × 15 observation items on the COI × an average of 2.5 observer comments per item). To reduce the overwhelming quantity of data, they were *quantitized*. COI field notes were analyzed by independent raters. Considering all notes for any given teacher, two raters scored each of the indicators of effective teaching from 1 (strong evidence of effective teaching) to 2 (contradictory evidence) to 3 (effective teaching not evident). The results of the statistical analyses (*t*-tests and MANOVA/ANOVA) indicated that teachers in more effective schools did indeed demonstrate much higher quality teaching than those in less effective schools.

This portion of the LSES was a Type I mixed model design. The study was confirmatory, with hypotheses set up in advance predicting that more effective schools would be characterized by teachers who provided higher quality instruction than teachers in less effective schools. The data collection and operations were purely qualitative, with observer responses to the COI generating a large amount of narrative data in the form of field notes. The analyses were quantitative, using standard statistical analyses on data that had been converted to numbers using quantitizing techniques.

Type II Mixed Design: Confirmatory Investigation, Qualitative Data/Operations, Qualitative Analysis and Inference

Another aspect of the Teddlie et al. (1989) research involved the use of the case study approach to further understand the processes whereby more effective teaching occurs in more effective schools and less effective teaching occurs in less effective schools. A finding of the study was that the teachers in more effective schools displayed more consistent behaviors (i.e., the standard deviation of their behaviors was smaller) than teachers from less effective schools. One purpose for examining the qualitative data was to determine how these differences in the behavior of teachers (i.e., both the mean and the variance differences) occurred.

The LSES-III qualitative data consisted of the field notes taken while observing throughout the school and in the classrooms as well as the interviews conducted with the principal and the teachers. The researchers selected one matched pair of schools in which the differences in quality of teaching between the two schools was quite large. The researchers then examined the field notes from these two schools closely to try to determine the differential ongoing processes. Their qualitative descriptions were included in the results section of Teddlie et al. (1989) and focused on the principals at the differentially effective schools: One was a proactive "guardian" of academic time at her school, while the other allowed academic time to "slip through the fingers of the faculty."

This portion of the LSES was a confirmatory study, with hypotheses set up in advance predicting that more effective schools would be characterized by teachers who provided higher quality instruction than teachers in less effective schools. The data collection and operations were purely qualitative, consisting of the field notes taken while observing throughout the school and in the classrooms as well as the interviews conducted with the principal and the teachers. The analyses and inferences were qualitative, using inductively oriented methods in which the field notes were examined for emerging themes that would describe the processes underlying the statistical differences that had previously been uncovered.

Type III Mixed Design: Exploratory Investigation, Quantitative Data/Operations, Statistical Analysis and Inference

The Stringfield and Teddlie (1990) study, described above as using a purely qualitative design, also employed a Type III mixed design at the insistence of the editors of *School Effectiveness and School Improvement,* who required that the researchers look at quantitative data and analyses before they would publish the purely qualitative results. These editors wanted to be sure that the investigators were observing "real" school improvement, and they insisted that the researchers provide "hard" data to that effect (i.e., standardized test data indicating that the schools were scoring better than they had done in the past).

Thus, ex post facto, the researchers examined CRT and NRT data for the schools, using information from the 1982-1984, 1984-1985, and 1989-1990 school years. The results from these quantitative data were congruent with the previously gathered qualitative data, confirming that some type of improvement was occurring in the four schools under study. This portion of the LSES was exploratory, given that no hypotheses regarding "naturally improving" school improvement had been set up in advance. The data collection and operations were quantitative, involving researcher-administered NRT and state-mandated CRT data. The analyses were statistical in nature, involving comparisons of data generated from the four improving schools with their previous test results and with results from their matched pairs.

Type IV Mixed Design: Exploratory Investigation, Qualitative Data/Operations, Statistical Analysis and Inference

Crone and Teddlie (1995) conducted a partial replication of previous research (e.g., Teddlie et al., 1989; Virgilio, Teddlie, & Oescher, 1991) regarding teacher behavior in differentially effective schools. In the interview component of this study, researchers queried teachers and principals regarding reasons for the different patterns of results found in teacher behavior in effective and ineffective schools: higher rates of effective teaching behavior and less variance in that behavior in more effective schools, and lower rates of effective teaching behavior and more variance in that behavior in less effective schools.

The researchers used an "interview guide approach" (Patton, 1990) in which topics and issues were specified in outline form in advance, which allowed the interviewers to determine the exact sequence and wording of the questions while the interview was ongoing. The topics were rather broad, concerning the selection and socialization of teachers, the cohesiveness of the faculties, the principals' implementation of change, and so on.

The researchers specified no hypotheses in advance for the interview component of the study, which was viewed as exploratory, designed to determine if teachers and principals in differentially effective schools viewed their experiences (e.g., selection and socialization) differently. The data gathered were narrative field notes taken in response to the open-ended questions from the interview guide.

As the researchers began to analyze the data using the constant comparative technique described by Lincoln and Guba (1985), a number of themes began to emerge. These themes appeared to be occurring with more or less frequency depending upon whether the interviewers were working in effective or ineffective schools. The researchers decided to count the different themes that emerged and then subject that numerical data to chi-square analyses.

This analysis technique is another example of the *quantitizing* methodology described in Chapter 6. Analysis of the interviews showed that

> there was more cohesiveness among the teachers in effective schools. . . . This included 13 teachers in effective schools and 14 teachers in ineffective schools. . . . All teachers were asked what kind of input they had regarding school goals. Twelve of the teachers in effective schools responded that teachers work together. Only two teachers in ineffective schools answered that teachers worked together on goals (Chi-square = 7.17, $p < .01$). (Crone & Teddlie, 1995, p. 5)

This component of the Crone and Teddlie (1995) study was a Type IV mixed model design. The study was exploratory, with no hypotheses set up in advance; the data collection and operations were qualitative, using interviews that resulted in narrative field notes; and the analyses and inferences were quantitative, employing chi-squares to analyze frequency count data that had been quantitized from the narrative data.

Type V Mixed Design: Confirmatory Investigation, Quantitative Data/Operations, Qualitative Analysis and Inference

Types V and VI mixed model designs are described as "rare" in Table 3.1. The major reason for this is that they involve the *qualitizing* methodology described in Chapter 6: converting quantitative data into narrative data that can then be analyzed qualitatively. While researchers in several of the behavioral and social sciences use the more common quantitizing techniques described in the Type I and IV mixed model studies above, fewer researchers have experience in using the qualitizing methodology to generate profiles and categories.

A recent example of the use of this technique in a confirmatory study is the research of Durland and Teddlie (Durland, 1996; Durland & Teddlie, 1996), which involved the analysis of sociometric data from LSES-IV. Sociometric questionnaires generate data that are inherently mixed: quantitative data in the form of sociomatrices (numerical indices) and qualitative data in the form of sociograms (two-dimensional drawings of relationships among social units).

Sociometric questions typically are very simple; for example, in LSES-IV, the primary question asked faculty members to indicate and rank the top three individuals with whom they had communicated about academic matters in the past two weeks. From this simple question, very complex quantitative sociomatrices (e.g., numerical measures of centrality for the principal, numerical measures of cohesiveness and density for the faculty) as well as qualitative sociograms (pictures of the faculty interaction patterns, including cliques, isolates, and so on) can be generated. In LSES-IV, both sociomatrices and sociograms were used, but it can be asserted that the sociograms produced the most valuable information. The sociograms allowed the confirmation of predictions regarding the interaction patterns that should exist in effective and ineffective schools based on the extant school effectiveness research.

Durland (1996) developed a model, the Centrality-Cohesiveness Model of School Effectiveness, that predicted the types of sociogram patterns she expected from schools varying in terms of a school effectiveness index (SEI; effective or ineffective) and SES of student body (middle or low). These predicted sociograms, or visual representations of faculty inter-actions, were based on SER theory and research regarding the types of leaders and communication patterns that one might expect to find in such schools. This study used an advanced computer program, KrackPlot (Krackhardt, Lundberg, & O'Rourke, 1993), to generate the sociograms based on the empirical data. The researchers then compared the empirically derived sociograms with the theoretically derived ones that had been predicted in advance.

The sociogram analyses indicated that (a) effective schools were more likely to be dense and centralized ("well webbed"), while ineffective schools were more likely to be spread out and linear ("stringy"); (b) the principal, or surrogate leader, was more likely to be in the center of sociograms of effective schools than ineffective schools, where they tended to be located on the periphery; and (c) there were more isolates and cliques in ineffective as opposed to effective schools.

This component of the LSES-IV study was confirmatory, with hypotheses set up in advance predicting certain types of interaction patterns among faculty members based on the extant SER literature. The data collection and operations were quantitative, with the use of sociometric questionnaires to ask faculty members to rank individuals in their schools in terms of how much they interacted with them. The analyses and inferences for the described component of the study were qualitative, using a computer program (KrackPlot) to generate pictures of the faculty interaction patterns in effective and ineffective schools based on the empirical, numerical data.

Type VI Mixed Design: Exploratory Investigation, Quantitative Data/Operations, Qualitative Analysis and Inference

The LSES-IV study also generated an example of an exploratory study that used the qualitizing technique. As indicated in Table 8.1, LSES-IV was a five-year follow-up study of eight matched pairs of schools. These schools had been initially classified as effective or ineffective based on baseline data from school years 1982-1983 and 1983-1984; their effectiveness status was confirmed through site visits conducted in LSES-III in 1984-1985. While all the schools retained their initial classification status in LSES-III, there was evidence of some naturally occurring school improvement, which was described earlier.

The researchers anticipated that by the time of LSES-IV, some of the 16 schools might be different in terms of their effectiveness status, but they decided *not* to make predictions in advance regarding these changes. In fact, the researchers were not even sure if the initial dichotomous classification scheme (effective/ineffective) would be adequate to characterize the schools as they had evolved by the time of LSES-IV in 1989-1990.

Instead of predicting the status of the schools in LSES-IV, the researchers decided to use a multidimensional set of quantitative criteria to determine the effectiveness status, and indeed effectiveness categories, for the schools. Teddlie and Stringfield (1993, pp. 84-85) presented data on eight quantitative criteria for each of the schools: scores on criterion-referenced tests, scores on norm-referenced tests, student attendance, scores on high-inference measures of the quality of classroom teaching, time-on-task in classrooms, stability of faculty, scores on a researcher-completed measure of the overall school climate (hierarchical dimensions of schooling), and changes in the socioeconomic status of the student bodies of the schools.

Based on these quantitative data, the researchers developed a new scheme for categorizing the schools into four qualitatively defined categories: stable more effective, improving, declining, and stable less effective. This component of the LSES-IV study was exploratory, with no hypotheses set up in advance regarding the categories of effectiveness that might emerge. The data collection and operations were quantitative, with the use of eight separate numerical indices of effectiveness. The analyses and inferences were qualitative, using the qualitizing technique whereby numerical data were transformed into narrative descriptions (case studies) of the 16 schools, which then were analyzed qualitatively to produce four emerging categories.

9

Conclusions and
Future Directions

A major purpose of this volume has been to extend the philosophical and methodological "bridges" that are under construction between the QUAL and QUAN research traditions. Both research traditions are very rich and have ardent supporters, some of whom have expended much effort over the past two decades to keep them separated. This effort at reconciliation has been challenging but at the same time rewarding. We had to cover material in several diverse areas, from philosophical foundations to "hands-on examples" of actual research in the field. We hope that we were able to demonstrate that mixing the QUAN and QUAL approaches to research is not only possible but also quite beneficial in many diverse research settings. This point is specifically relevant to graduate students, who are often uncertain about using mixed methods in their dissertation research.

A second point that we have emphasized throughout this volume is the preeminence of the *research question* over considerations of either method or paradigm. We discussed this early in the volume under the title of "the dictatorship of the question." The question determines the design of the study, the data collection approach, and so on. The best method is the one that answers the research question(s) most efficiently, and with foremost inference quality (trustworthiness, internal validity). Mixed methods are often more efficient in answering research questions than either the QUAL or the QUAN approach alone. We often hear graduate students say, "If I am going to do my dissertation research using qualitative methods, why should I learn quantitative methods and statistics?" A similar question is asked by students who prefer quantitative methods. We hope this volume has provided some answers for both groups of students through its emphasis on the importance of research questions and on the superiority of mixed methods in reaching comprehensive answers to those questions.

One of the conclusions of this volume is that the paradigm of pragmatism can be employed as the philosophical underpinning for using mixed methods and mixed models, especially with regard to issues of epistemology, axiology, and ontology. Pragmatism rejects the "either-or" decision points associated with the paradigm wars. We also emphasized that a taxonomy of mixed methods and mixed models is needed, due to the conceptual confusion that currently characterizes literature in the area. We first proposed a typology of monomethods, mixed methods, and mixed model studies. We then derived a typology for mixed model designs that is based on three basic dimensions, or stages, of the research process: type of investigation (exploratory or confirmatory), type of data collection and operations (QUAN or QUAL), and type of analysis and inference (qualitative or statistical). These typologies are tentative and were put forward to stimulate conversation among research methodologists about the best way to organize mixed method and mixed model studies.

We tried to demonstrate, within space limitations, that a growing number of researchers in the social and behavioral sciences are using the eight mixed model designs (six simple and two more complex) in which the QUAN and QUAL approaches are mixed across all phases of the research process. In many cases, researchers are using these models with little awareness that they are mixed. From these examples, one might conclude that complex mixed models (Types VII and VIII) appear to be used more often by sophisticated researchers than the simpler mixed models (Types I-VI). For novice researchers, it is probably better to start by using the simpler mixed models.

We tried to build a bridge between the QUAL and QUAN approaches with regard to questions of inference quality (internal validity/trustworthiness). Because this is an issue of great relevance to all researchers, we strongly believe that evaluation of the internal validity/trustworthiness of inferences is a critical issue to be reconciled between the two approaches. As a part of our teaching research methodology, we often ask our students to critically evaluate research reports from different disciplines. The *most* important problem that *they* almost always identify involves the interpretation of the results for making conclusions. We are confident that many of our colleagues receive similar feedback from their students.

The issue is not unique to either of the two (QUAL/QUAN) approaches. An examination of the conclusion section of journal articles readily demonstrates this point. Some researchers in both the QUAN and the QUAL traditions inappropriately generalize beyond what their data warrant by expressing conclusions that (a) are not internally valid, because they are based on interpretation of relationships that have possible alternative explanations, or (b) are not trustworthy, because adequate credibility techniques (e.g., prolonged engagement, persistent observation, member checks) have not been established.

We believe that a good research report should help the reader draw conclusions with some degree of certainty. A researcher's role is to provide the means for achieving such certainty in making inferences on the basis of the results. The quality of an investigator's inferences regarding the relationship between the variables under study depends on how certain the researcher *and* the informed reader of the results are that no strong plausible explanations, other than the one set forth, exist.

There are suspicions, and misunderstandings, regarding both approaches to research. Much of quantitative research is criticized for emphasizing the statistical significance (probability of obtaining a relationship by chance) at the expense of focusing on the magnitude of the relationship/effect. QUAN studies are also criticized for failure to incorporate a broader range of information, such as observations and unstructured responses, in their analysis. Even when such data are collected, they are often reduced to simple categories through quantitizing. QUAL researchers, on the other hand, are often criticized for their selectivity in reporting the results (often a function of the fact that no simple data reduction method is available for reporting), for not providing "alternative perspectives to increase the credibility of findings" (Murphy & O'Leary, 1994, p. 214), and for expressing personal opinions instead of accurately reflecting the perspectives of their informants.

Many of these misunderstandings (or sometimes correctly diagnosed problems!) can easily be alleviated through the use of mixed research methods and a rigorous evaluation of the internal validity and trustworthiness of the findings obtained through such methods. Triangulation techniques, involving the reconciliation of QUAL and QUAN data sources, provide the lynchpin for improving the quality of inferences.

References

Aghajanian, A., & Moghadas, A. A. (in press). Trends, correlates and consequences of divorce in Iran. *Journal of Divorce and Remarriage, 29.*

Ary, D., Jacobs, L. C., & Razavieh, A. (1996). *Introduction to research in education* (5th ed.). Fort Worth: Harcourt Brace College.

Babbie, E. (1992). *The practice of social research.* Belmont, CA: Wadsworth.

Bacharach, S., Bauer, S. C., & Shedd, J. B. (1986). *The learning workplace: The conditions and resources of teaching.* (ERIC Document Reproduction Service No. ED 279 614)

Bannister, R. C. (1987). *Sociology and scientism: The American quest for objectivity, 1890-1940.* Berkeley: University of California Press.

Barnett, D. W., & Macmann, G. M. (1990). Personality assessment: Critical issues for research and practice. In C. R. Reynolds & R. W. Kamphaus (Eds.), *Handbook of psychological and educational assessment of children* (Vol. 2). New York: Guilford.

Berelson, B. (1952). *Content analysis in communication research.* Glencoe, IL: Free Press.

Bernstein, R. (1983). *Beyond objectivism and relativism.* Philadelphia: University of Pennsylvania Press.

Blalock, H. M. (1978). Ordering diversity. *Society, 15,* 20-22.

Bogdan, R. C., & Biklen, S. J. (1982). *Qualitative research for education: An introduction to theory and method.* Boston: Allyn & Bacon.

Brewer, J., & Hunter, A. (1989). *Multimethod research: A synthesis of styles.* Newbury Park, CA: Sage.

Brien, T. M., Dennis, L. T., Mahoney, C. A., & Wallnau, L. (1994). Dimensions of self-efficacy among three groups of condom users. *Journal of American College Health, 42,* 167-174.

Brookover, W. B., Beady, C., Flood, P., Schweitzer, J., & Wisenbaker, J. (1979). *Schools, social systems and student achievement: Schools can make a difference.* New York: Praeger.

Brown, S., Riddell, S., & Duffield, J. (1996). Possibilities and problems of small-scale studies to unpack the findings of large-scale studies of school effectiveness. In J. Gray, D. Reynolds, C. Fitz-Gibbon, & D. Jesson (Eds.), *Merging traditions: The future of research on school effectiveness and school improvement* (pp. 93-120). London: Cassell.

Bryk, A. S., & Raudenbush, S. W. (1992). *Hierarchical linear models.* Newbury Park, CA: Sage.

Campbell, D., & Fiske, D. W. (1959). Convergent and discriminant validation by the multitrait-multimethod matrix. *Psychological Bulletin, 54,* 297-312.

Campbell, D.T., & Stanley, J. (1966). *Experimental and quasi-experimental design for research.* Chicago: Rand McNally.

171

Caracelli, V. W., & Greene, J. C. (1993). Data analysis strategies for mixed-method evaluation designs. *Educational Evaluation and Policy Analysis, 15*(2), 195-207.

Carey, J. W. (1993). Linking qualitative and quantitative methods: Integrating cultural factors into public health. *Qualitative Health Research, 3,* 298-318.

Chandler, L. A. (1990). The projective hypothesis and the development of projective techniques for children. In C. R. Reynolds & R. W. Kamphaus (Eds.), *Handbook of psychological and educational assessment of children* (Vol. 2). New York: Guilford.

Cherryholmes, C. C. (1992). Notes on pragmatism and scientific realism. *Educational Researcher, 21,* 13-17.

Chrispeels, J. H. (1992). *Purposeful restructuring: Creating a culture for learning and achievement in elementary schools.* London: Falmer.

Cook, T. D., & Campbell, D. T. (1979). *Quasiexperimentation: Design and analysis issues for field settings.* Boston: Houghton Mifflin.

Creswell, J. W. (1995). *Research design: Qualitative and quantitative approaches.* Thousand Oaks, CA: Sage.

Cronbach, L. J. (1982). *Designing evaluations of educational and social programs.* San Francisco: Jossey-Bass.

Crone, L., & Teddlie, C. (1995). Further examination of teacher behavior in differentially effective schools: Selection and socialization processes. *Journal of Classroom Interaction, 30*(1), 1-9.

Datta, L. (1994). Paradigm wars: A basis for peaceful coexistence and beyond. In C. S. Reichardt & S. F. Rallis (Eds.), *The qualitative-quantitative debate: New perspectives* (pp. 53-70). San Francisco: Jossey-Bass.

Davidson, D. (1973). On the very idea of a conceptual scheme. *Proceedings of the American Philosophical Association, 68,* 5-20.

Denzin, N. K. (1978). The logic of naturalistic inquiry. In N. K. Denzin (Ed.), *Sociological methods: A sourcebook.* New York: McGraw-Hill.

Denzin, N. K. (1992). *Symbolic interactionism and cultural studies.* Cambridge: Basil Blackwell.

Denzin, N. K., & Lincoln, Y. S. (Eds.). (1994). *Handbook of qualitative research.* Thousand Oaks, CA: Sage.

DeVellis, R. F. (1991). *Scale development: Theory and applications.* Newbury Park, CA: Sage.

Dooley, D. (1995). *Social research methods* (3rd ed.). Englewood Cliffs, NJ: Prentice Hall.

Dressler, W. W. (1991). *Stress and adaptation in the context of culture: Depression in a southern black community.* Albany: State University of New York Press.

Durland, M. (1996). *The application of network analysis to the study of differentially effective schools.* Unpublished doctoral dissertation, Louisiana State University, Baton Rouge.

Durland, M., & Teddlie, C. (1996, April). *A network analysis of the structural dimensions of principal leadership in differentially effective schools.* Paper presented at the annual meeting of the American Educational Research Association, New York.

Duval, S., & Wicklund, R. A. (1972). *A theory of objective self-awareness.* New York: Academic Press.

Eisner, E. W. (1975). *The perceptive eye: Toward the formulation of educational evaluation* (Occasional Papers of the Stanford Evaluation Consortium). Stanford, CA: Stanford University Press.

Eisner, E. W. (1991). *The enlightened eye: Qualitative inquiry and the enhancement of educational practice*. New York: Macmillan.

Fals-Stewart, W., Birchler, G., Schafer, J., & Lucente, S. (1994). The personality of marital distress: An empirical typology. *Journal of Personality Assessment, 62,* 223-241.

Fetterman, D. M. (1992). In response to Lee Sechrest's 1991 AEA presidential address: "Roots: Back to our first generations," February 1991, 1-7. *Evaluation Practice, 13,* 171-172.

Floyd, J. A. (1993). The use of across-method triangulation in the study of sleep concerns in healthy older adults. *Advances-in-Nursing-Science, 16*(2), 70-80.

Fowler, F. J. (1993). *Survey research methods*. Newbury Park, CA: Sage.

Fowler, F. J., & Mangione, T. W. (1990). *Standardizing interviewer-related error.* Newbury Park, CA: Sage.

Franklin, R. D., Allison, D. B., & Gorman, B. S. (1996). *Design and analysis of single case research*. Mahwah, NJ: Lawrence Erlbaum.

Freeman, D. (1983). *Margaret Mead and Samoa: The making and unmaking of an anthropological myth*. Cambridge, MA: Harvard University Press.

Freeman, J., & Teddlie, C. (1996, April). *A phenomenological examination of "naturally occurring" school improvement: Implications for democratization of schools*. Paper presented at the annual meeting of the American Educational Research Association, New York.

Gage, N. (1989). The paradigm wars and their aftermath: A "historical" sketch of research and teaching since 1989. *Educational Researcher, 18,* 4-10.

Gall, M. D., Borg, W. R., & Gall, J. P. (1996). *Educational research: An introduction* (6th ed.). New York: Longman.

Gardner, M. (1993). The great Samoan hoax. *Skeptical Inquirer, 17,* 131-135.

Geertz, C. (1973). *The interpretation of culture*. New York: Basic Books.

Gergen, K. J. (1973). Social psychology as history. *Journal of Personality and Social Psychology, 26,* 309-320.

Gergen, K. J. (1985). The social constructionist movement in modern psychology. *American Psychologist, 40,* 266-275.

Glaser, B. G., & Strauss, A. L. (1967). *The discovery of grounded theory: Strategies for qualitative research*. Chicago: Aldine.

Goetz, J. P., & LeCompte, M. D. (1984). *Ethnography and qualitative design in educational research*. New York: Academic Press.

Goodman, N. (1984). *Of mind and other matters*. Cambridge, MA: Harvard University Press.

Gravetter, F. J., & Wallnau, L. B. (1998). *Statistics for the behavioral sciences*. St. Paul, MN: West.

Greenberg, J., & Folger, R. (1988). *Controversial issues in social research methods*. New York: Springer-Verlag.

Greene, J. C. (1994). Qualitative program evaluation. In N. K. Denzin & Y. S. Lincoln (Eds.), *Handbook of qualitative research* (pp. 530-544). Thousand Oaks, CA: Sage.

Greene, J. C., Caracelli, V. J., & Graham, W. F. (1989). Toward a conceptual framework for mixed-method evaluation designs. *Educational Evaluation and Policy Analysis, 11,* 255-274.

Guba, E. G. (1987). What have we learned about naturalistic evaluation? *Evaluation Practice, 8,* 23-43.

Guba, E. G. (1990). *The paradigm dialog*. Newbury Park, CA: Sage.

Guba, E. G., & Lincoln, Y. S. (1990). *Fourth-generation evaluation*. Newbury Park, CA: Sage.

Guba, E. G., & Lincoln, Y. S. (1994). Competing paradigms in qualitative research. In N. K. Denzin & Y. S. Lincoln (Eds.), *Handbook of qualitative research* (pp. 105-117). Thousand Oaks, CA: Sage.

Haak, R. A. (1990). Using sentence completion to assess emotional disturbance. In C. R. Reynolds & R. W. Kamphaus (Eds.), *Handbook of psychological and educational assessment of children* (Vol. 2). New York: Guilford.

Hallinger, P., & Murphy, J. (1986). The social context of effective schools. *American Journal of Education, 94,* 328-355.

Hammersley, M. (1989). *The dilemma of qualitative method: Herbert Blumer and the Chicago tradition*. London: Routledge Kegan Paul.

Hammersley, M. (1992). *What's wrong with ethnography*. London: Routledge Kegan Paul.

Hanson, N. R. (1958). *Patterns of discovery: An inquiry into the conceptual foundations of science*. Cambridge: Cambridge University Press.

Harris, R. (1985). *A primer of multivariate statistics*. Orlando, FL: Academic Press.

Hedrick, T. E., Bickman, L., & Rog, D. J. (1993). *Applied research design: A practical guide*. Newbury Park, CA: Sage.

Henry, G. T. (1990). *Practical sampling*. Newbury Park, CA: Sage.

Hooper, M. L. (1994). The effects of high and low level cognitive and literacy language arts tasks on motivation and learning in multiability, multicultural classrooms. *Developmental Studies: Learning-and-Instruction, 4*(3), 233-251.

House, E. R. (1994). Integrating the quantitative and qualitative. In C. S. Reichardt & S. F. Rallis (Eds.), *The qualitative-quantitative debate: New perspectives* (pp. 13-22). San Francisco: Jossey-Bass.

Howe, K. R. (1988). Against the quantitative-qualitative incompatibility thesis or dogmas die hard. *Educational Researcher, 17,* 10-16.

Huberman, A. M., & Miles, M. B. (1994). Data management and analysis methods. In N. K. Denzin & Y. S. Lincoln (Eds.), *Handbook of qualitative research* (pp. 428-444). Thousand Oaks, CA: Sage.

Hughes, J. N., Barker, D., Kemenoff, S., & Hart, M. (1996). Problem ownership, causal attributions, and self-efficacy as predictors of teachers' referral decisions. *Journal of Educational and Psychological Consultation, 4,* 369-384.

Ingles, S. J., Scott, L. A., Lindmark, J. T., Frankel, M. R., Myers, S. L., & Wu, S. (1992). *National Education Longitudinal Study of 1988: First follow-up: Student component data file user manual* (Vol. 1). Washington, DC: U.S. Department of Education.

Iwanicki, E. E., & Tashakkori, A. (1994). *The proficiencies of the effective principal: A validation study*. Baton Rouge: Louisiana Department of Education.

Janesick, V. J. (1994). The dance of qualitative research design: Metaphor, methodolatry, and meaning. In N. K. Denzin & Y. S. Lincoln (Eds.), *Handbook of qualitative research* (pp. 209-219). Thousand Oaks, CA: Sage.

Jick, T. D. (1979). Mixing qualitative and quantitative methods: Triangulation in action. *Administrative Science Quarterly, 24,* 602-611.

Jimenez, R. T., Garcia, G. E., & Pearson, P. D. (1995). Three children, two languages, and strategic learning: Case studies in bilingual/monolingual reading. *American Educational Research Journal, 32,* 67-98.

Joffe, A., & Radius, S. M. (1993). Self-efficacy and intent to use condoms among entering college freshmen. *Journal of Adolescent Health, 14,* 262-268.

Johnson, M. J., & Pajares, F. (1996). When shared decision making works: A 3-year longitudinal study. *American Educational Research Journal, 33,* 599-627.

Jones, E. E., & Davis, K. E. (1966). From acts to dispositions: The attribution process in person perception. In L. Berkowitz (Ed.), *Advances in experimental social psychology* (Vol. 2). New York: Freeman.

Jones, E. E., & Nisbett, R. E. (1972). The actor and the observer: Divergent perceptions of the causes of behavior. In E. E. Jones, D. E. Kanouse, H. H. Kelley, E. E. Nisbett, S. Valins, & B. Weiner (Eds.), *Attributions: Perceiving the causes of behavior.* Morristown, NJ: General Learning Press.

Keirsey, D., & Bates, M. (1984). *Please understand me: Character and temperament types.* Del Mar, CA: Prometheus Nemesis.

Kerlinger, F. N. (1986). *Foundations of behavioral research.* New York: Holt, Rinehart & Winston.

Kidder, L. H. (1981). Qualitative research and quasi-experimental frameworks. In M. B. Brewer & B. E. Collins (Eds.), *Scientific inquiry and the social sciences.* San Francisco: Jossey-Bass.

Kneller, G. F. (1984). *Movements of thought in modern education.* New York: John Wiley.

Knoff, H. M. (1990). Evaluation of projective drawings. In C. R. Reynolds & R. W. Kamphaus (Eds.), *Handbook of psychological and educational assessment of children* (Vol. 2). New York: Guilford.

Kochan, S., Tashakkori, A., & Teddlie, C. (1996, April). *You can't judge a high school by achievement alone: Preliminary findings from the construction of behavioral indicators of school effectiveness.* Paper presented at the annual meeting of the American Educational Research Association, New York.

Krackhardt, D., Lundberg, M., & O'Rourke, L. (1993). KrackPlot: A picture's worth a thousand words. *Connections, 16,* 37-47.

Krathwohl, D. R. (1993). *Methods of educational and social science research: An integrated approach.* White Plains, NY: Longman.

Krueger, R. A. (1988). *Focus groups: A practical guide for applied research.* Newbury Park, CA: Sage.

Kuhn, T. S. (1970). *The structure of scientific revolutions* (2nd ed.). Chicago: University of Chicago Press.

Latane, B., & Rodin, J. (1969). A lady in distress: Inhibiting effects of friends and strangers on bystander intervention. *Journal of Experimental Social Psychology, 5,* 189-202.

Lavrakas, P. J. (1993). *Telephone survey methods: Sampling, selection, and supervision.* Newbury Park, CA: Sage.

LeCompte, M. D., & Preissle, J., with Tesch, R. (1993). *Ethnography and qualitative design in educational research* (2nd ed.). New York: Academic Press.

Leininger, M. M. (1985). *Qualitative research methods in nursing.* New York: Grune & Stratton.

Lincoln, Y. S. (1991). The arts and sciences of program evaluation. *Evaluation Practice, 12,* 1-7.

Lincoln, Y. S., & Guba, E.G. (1985). *Naturalistic inquiry.* Beverly Hills, CA: Sage.

Mangione, T. W. (1995). *Mail surveys: Improving the quality.* Thousand Oaks, CA: Sage.

Mann, A. F. (1994). College peer tutoring: Maps of development. *Journal of College Student Development, 35,* 164-169.

Manning, P. K., & Cullum-Swan, B. (1994). Narrative, content, and semiotic analysis. In N. K. Denzin & Y. S. Lincoln (Eds.), *Handbook of qualitative research* (pp. 463-477). Thousand Oaks, CA: Sage.

Marin, G., & Marin, V. M. (1991). *Research with Hispanic populations*. Newbury Park, CA: Sage.

Marsh, H. W. (1994). Using the National Longitudinal Study of 1988 to evaluate theoretical models of self concept: The Self-Description Questionnaire. *Journal of Educational Psychology, 86,* 439-456.

Maruyama, G., & Deno, S. (1992). *Research in educational settings*. Newbury Park, CA: Sage.

Maxwell, J. A. (1996). *Qualitative research design: An interpretive approach*. Thousand Oaks, CA: Sage.

McMillan, J. H. (1996). *Educational research: Fundamentals for the consumer* (2nd ed.). New York: HarperCollins

McMillan, J. H., & Schumacher, S. (1997). *Research in education*. New York: Longman.

McNamara, J. F. (1994).*Surveys and experiments in education research*. Basel, Switzerland: Technomic.

Meekers, D. (1994). Combining ethnographic and survey methods: A study of the nuptiality patterns of the Shona of Zimbabwe. *Journal of Comparative Family Studies, 25*(3), 313-328.

Miles, M., & Huberman, M. (1994). *Qualitative data analysis: An expanded sourcebook* (2nd ed.). Thousand Oaks, CA: Sage.

Miller, W. L., & Crabtree, B. J. (1994). Clinical research. In N. K. Denzin & Y. S. Lincoln (Eds.), *Handbook of qualitative research* (pp. 340-352). Thousand Oaks, CA: Sage.

Mishler, E. G. (1990). Validation in inquiry-guided research: The role of examples in narrative studies. *Harvard Educational Review, 60,* 415-441.

Morse, J. M. (1991). Approaches to qualitative-quantitative methodological triangulation. *Nursing Research, 40,* 120-123.

Murphy, C. M., & O'Leary, K. D. (1994). Research paradigms, values, and spouse abuse. *Journal of Interpersonal Violence, 9,* 207-223.

Murphy, J. P. (1990). *Pragmatism: From Peirce to Davidson*. Boulder, CO: Westview.

Nielsen, K. (1991). *After the demise of the tradition: Rorty, critical theory, and the fate of philosophy*. Boulder, CO: Westview.

Patton, M. Q. (1990). *Qualitative evaluation and research methods* (2nd ed.). Newbury Park, CA: Sage.

Pemberton, M. B., Insko, C. A., & Schopler, J. (1996). Memory for and experience of differential competitive behavior of individuals and groups. *Journal of Personality and Social Psychology, 71,* 953-966.

Phillips, D. C. (1990). Postpositivist science: Myths and realities. In E. Guba (Ed.), *The paradigm dialog*. Newbury Park, CA: Sage.

Popper, K. R. (1959). *The logic of scientific discovery*. New York: Basic Books.

Reichardt, C. S., & Rallis, S. F. (1994). Qualitative and quantitative inquiries are not incompatible: A call for a new partnership. In C. S. Reichardt & S. F. Rallis (Eds.), *The qualitative-quantitative debate: New perspectives* (pp. 85-92). San Francisco: Jossey-Bass.

Reis, H. R., & Wheeler, L. (1991). Studying social interaction with the Rochester interaction record. In M. P. Zanna (Ed.), *Advances in experimental social psychology* (Vol. 24, pp. 269-318). New York: Academic Press.

Richardson, L. (1994). Writing: A method of inquiry. In N. K. Denzin & Y. S. Lincoln (Eds.), *Handbook of qualitative research* (pp. 209-219). Thousand Oaks, CA: Sage.

Roberts, P., & Le-Dorze, G. (1994). Semantic verbal fluency in aphasia: A quantitative and qualitative study in test-retest conditions. *Aphasiology, 8*(6), 569-582.

Robinson, J. P., & Shaver, P. R. (1975). *Measures of social psychological attitudes.* Ann Arbor, MI: Institute for Social Research.

Robinson, J. P., Shaver, P. R., & Wrightsman, L. S. (1991). *Measures of personality and social psychological attitudes.* San Diego, CA: Academic Press.

Rorty, R. (1982). Pragmatism, relativism, and irrationalism. In R. Rorty (Ed.), *Consequences of pragmatism* (pp. 160-175). Minneapolis: University of Minnesota Press.

Rorty, R. (1990). Introduction. In J. P. Murphy (Ed.), *Pragmatism: From Peirce to Davidson.* Boulder, CO: Westview.

Rosenberg, M. (1979). *Conceiving the self.* New York: Basic Books.

Rosenshine, B. (1983). Teaching functions in instructional programs. *Elementary School Journal, 83,* 335-351.

Rosenshine, B., & Stevens, R. (1986). Teaching functions. In M. Wittrock (Ed.), *Third handbook of research on teaching.* New York: Macmillan.

Rosenthal, R. (1976). *Experimenter effects in behavioral research* (enlarged ed.). New York: Irvington.

Rosenthal, R. (1991). *Meta-analysis procedures for social research.* Newbury Park, CA: Sage.

Rosnow, R. R., & Rosenthal, R. (1996). *Beginning behavioral research: A conceptual primer* (2nd ed.). Englewood Cliffs, NJ: Prentice Hall.

Ross, D. (1991). *The origins of American social science.* Cambridge: Cambridge University Press.

Rossi, P. H. (1994). The war between the quals and quants: Is a lasting peace possible? In C. S. Reichardt & S. F. Rallis (Eds.), *The qualitative-quantitative debate: New perspectives* (pp. 23-36). San Francisco: Jossey-Bass.

Rusbult, C. E., Onizuka, R. K., & Lipkus, I. (1993). What do we really want? Mental models of ideal romantic involvement explored through multidimensional scaling. *Journal of Experimental Social Psychology, 29,* 493-527.

Salkind, N. J. (1997). *Exploring research.* Upper Saddle River, NJ: Prentice Hall.

Schuyten, S. (1995, April). *The effects of assessor and assessee gender, ethnicity, and assessor's role on performance assessment of teachers.* Unpublished doctoral dissertation, Louisiana State University, Baton Rouge.

Schuyten, S., & Tashakkori, A. (1995). *Effects of assessor and assessee gender and ethnicity, and assessor's role on performance assessment of teachers.* Paper presented at the annual meeting of the American Educational Research Association, San Francisco.

Schwandt, T. A. (1994). Constructivist, interpretivist approaches to human inquiry. In N. K. Denzin & Y. S. Lincoln (Eds.), *Handbook of qualitative research* (pp. 118-137). Thousand Oaks, CA: Sage.

Sechrest, L. (1991). Roots: Back to our first generations. *Evaluation Practice, 13,* 1-7.

Sechrest, L., & Sidani, S. (1995). Quantitative and qualitative methods: Is there an alternative? *Evaluation and Program Planning, 18*(1), 77-87.

Shadish, W. R. (1995). Philosophy of science and the quantitative-qualitative debates: Thirteen common errors. *Evaluation and Program Planning, 18,* 63-75.

Sinclair, A. (1994). Prediction-making as an instructional strategy: Implications of teacher effects on learning, attitude toward science, and classroom practices. *Journal of Research and Development in Education, 27,* 153-161.

Smith, J. K. (1983). Quantitative versus qualitative research: An attempt to clarify the issue. *Educational Researcher, 12,* 6-13.

Smith, J. K., & Heshusius, L. (1986). Closing down the conversation: The end of the quantitative-qualitative debate among educational researchers. *Educational Researcher, 15*, 4-12.

Smith, M. L. (1994). Qualitative plus/versus quantitative: The last word. In C. S. Reichardt & S. F. Rallis (Eds.), *The qualitative-quantitative debate: New perspectives* (pp. 37-44). San Francisco: Jossey-Bass.

Smith, T. E., Sells, S. P., & Clevenger, T. (1994). Ethnographic content analysis of couple and therapist perceptions in a reflecting team setting. *Journal of Marital and Family Therapy, 20*(3), 267-286.

Spradley, J. P. (1979). *The ethnographic interview.* New York: Holt, Rinehart & Winston.

Spradley, J. P. (1980). *Participant observation.* New York: Holt, Rinehart & Winston.

Stallings, J. A. (1980). Allocated academic learning time revisited, or beyond time on task. *Educational Researcher, 9*(11), 11-16.

Stallings, J. A., & Kaskowitz, D. (1974). *Follow through classroom observation evaluation (1972-1973).* Menlo Park, CA: SRT International.

Stange, K. C., & Zyzanski, S. J. (1989). Integrating qualitative and quantitative research methods. *Family Medicine, 21*, 448-451.

Stevens, J. P. (1996). *Applied multivariate statistics for the social sciences.* Mahwah, NJ: Lawrence Erlbaum.

Stewardt, D. W., & Shamdasani, P. N. (1990). *Focus groups: Theory and practice.* Newbury Park, CA: Sage.

Stewart, D. W., & Kamins, M. A. (1993). *Secondary research: Information sources and methods* (2nd ed.). Newbury Park, CA: Sage.

Stringfield, S. (1994). Outlier studies of school effectiveness. In D. Reynolds, B. Creemers, P. Nesserlrodt, E. Schaffer, S. Stringfield, & C. Teddlie, *Advances in school effectiveness research and practice.* Oxford: Pergamon.

Stringfield, S., & Teddlie, C. (1990). School improvement efforts: Qualitative and quantitative data from four naturally occurring experiments in Phases III and IV of the Louisiana School Effectiveness Study. *School Effectiveness and School Improvement, 1*(2), 139-162.

Stringfield, S., & Teddlie, C. (1991). Observers as predictors of schools' effectiveness status. *Elementary School Journal, 91*(4), 357-376.

Takane, Y., Young, F. W., & DeLeeuw, J. (1977). Nonmetric individual difference multidimensional scaling: An alternative least squares method with optimal scaling features. *Psychometrika, 42*, 7-67.

Tashakkori, A. (1993). Gender, ethnicity, and the structure of self-esteem: An attitude theory approach. *Journal of Social Psychology, 4*, 479-488.

Tashakkori, A., Aghajanian, A., & Mehryar, A. H. (1996, July). *Consistency of Iranian adolescent behavioral intentions across two decades of change.* Paper presented at the 54th Annual Convention of the International Council of Psychologists, Banf, Alberta, Canada.

Tashakkori, A., Boyd, R., & Sines, M. (1996, July). *Predictors of drop-out and persistence of 8th grade Hispanic youth in the U.S.* Paper presented at the 54th Annual Convention of the International Council of Psychologists, Banf, Alberta, Canada.

Tashakkori, A., Haghighat, S., & Yousefi, F. (1990). Effects of preschool education on intelligence and achievement of a group of Iranian elementary school children. *International Review of Education, 34*, 499-508.

Tashakkori, A., & Thompson, V. D. (1991). Social change and change in intentions of Iranian youth regarding education, marriage, and careers. *International Journal of Psychology, 26,* 885-893.

Tashakkori, A., Thompson, V. D., & Mehryar, A. H. (1987). Iranian adolescents' intended age of marriage and desired family size. *Journal of Marriage and the Family, 49,* 917-924.

Taylor, D. L., & Tashakkori, A. (1995). Participation in decision making and school climate as predictors of teachers' job satisfaction and sense of efficacy. *Journal of Experimental Education, 63,* 217-230.

Taylor, D. L., & Tashakkori, A. (1997). Toward an understanding of teachers' desire for participation in decision making. *Journal of School Leadership, 7,* 1-20.

Taylor, D. L.,Tashakkori, A., & Hardwick, J. (1996, January). *Teachers' sense of efficacy and attributions for student success.* Paper presented at the annual meeting of the Southwestern Educational Research Association, New Orleans, LA.

Teddlie, C., Falkowski, C., Stringfield, S., Desselle, S., & Garvue, R. (1984). *The Louisiana School Effectiveness Study: Phase Two, 1982-84.* Baton Rouge: Louisiana State Department of Education. (Library of Congress call number: LA, 295, L877, 1984)

Teddlie, C., Kirby, P., & Stringfield, S. (1989). Effective versus ineffective schools: Observable differences in the classroom. *American Journal of Education, 97*(3), 221-236.

Teddlie, C., & Stringfield, S. (1993). *Schools make a difference: Lessons learned from a 10-year study of school effects.* New York: Teachers College Press.

Timberlake, E. M. (1994). Children with no place to call home: Survival in the cars and on the streets. *Child and Adolescent Social Work Journal, 11,* 259-278.

Trow, M. (1957). Comment on participant observation and interviewing: A comparison. *Human Organization, 16,* 33-35.

Udry, R. J., Dole, N., & Gleiter, K. (1992). Forming reproductive unions in urban Zimbabwe. *International Family Planning Perspectives, 18,* 10-12.

Ulin, P., Waszak, C., & Pfannenschmidt, S. (1996, November). *Integrating qualitative and quantitative research.* Paper presented at Family Health International's Women's Studies Project Technical Advisory Group Annual Meeting, Raleigh, NC.

Virgilio, I., Teddlie, C., & Oescher, J. (1991). Variance and context differences in teaching at differentially effective schools. *School Effectiveness and School Improvement, 2*(2), 152-168.

Wasserman, S., & Faust, K. (1994). *Social network analysis: Methods and applications.* Cambridge: Cambridge University Press.

Wetzler, S., Marlowe, D. B., & Sanderson, W. C. (1994). Assessment of depression using the MMPI, MILLON, and MILLON-II. *Psychological Reports, 75,* 755-768.

Whyte, W. F. (1943). *Street corner society.* Chicago: University of Chicago Press.

Wittgenstein, L. (1958). *The philosophical investigations* (2nd ed.). New York: Macmillan.

Wolcott, H. F. (1994). *Transforming qualitative data.* Thousand Oaks, CA: Sage.

Yin, R. K. (1993). *Case study research: Design and methods* (2nd ed.). Newbury Park, CA: Sage.

Yin, R. K. (1994). Evaluation: A singular craft. In C. S. Reichardt & S. F. Rallis (Eds.), *The qualitative-quantitative debate: New perspectives* (pp. 71-84). San Francisco: Jossey-Bass.

Index

About the Authors

Abbas Tashakkori is Professor of Educational Research Methodology at Louisiana State University. He received his Ph.D. in social psychology from the University of North Carolina—Chapel Hill in 1979. He has served on the psychology faculties of the Shiraz University (Iran), Stetson University, and Louisiana State University. He has been a Post-Doctoral Fellow of the Carolina Population Center at the University of North Carolina—Chapel Hill and a Visiting Scholar in the Department of Educational Administration at Texas A&M University. He has published numerous articles in national and international journals. His current scholarly work in progress include a coedited book titled *The Education of Hispanics in the US: Politics, Policies, and Outcomes*. Professors Tashakkori and Teddlie are currently planning the *Handbook of Mixed Model Research*.

Charles Teddlie is Professor of Educational Research Methodology at Louisiana State University. He received his Ph.D. in social psychology from the University of North Carolina—Chapel Hill in 1979 and thereafter served on the faculties of the University of New Orleans, the University of Newcastle-upon-Tyne (U.K.), and LSU. He also served as Assistant Superintendent for Research and Development at the Louisiana Department of Education. He has published more than 70 chapters and articles and is the coauthor or coeditor of six books, including *Schools Make a Difference: Lessons Learned From a 10-year Study of School Effects* (1993), *Forty Years After the Brown Decision: Social and Cultural Implications of School Desegregation* (1997), and *The International Handbook of School Effectiveness Research* (in press). He has lectured on school effectiveness research and educational research methodology in the United Kingdom, the Republic of Ireland, the Netherlands, Norway, Russia, the Ukraine, and Belarus.

APPLIED SOCIAL RESEARCH
METHODS SERIES
Series Editors
LEONARD BICKMAN, Peabody College, Vanderbilt University, Nashville
DEBRA J. ROG, Vanderbilt University, Washington, DC

Other volumes in this series are listed on the series page